ROD
OF THE
SPIRIT

DANNY LOVETT

21st CENTURY
PRESS

CHRISTIAN PUBLISHING WITH A PURPOSE
WWW.21STCENTURYPRESS.COM

ROD OF THE SPIRIT

Published by 21st Century Press

Springfield, MO 65807

21st Century Press
2131 W. Republic Rd.
PMB 41
Springfield, MO 65807

ISBN 0-9725719-6-5

Cover: Keith Locke
Book Design: Lee Fredrickson and Terry White

21ST CENTURY PRESS

CHRISTIAN PUBLISHING WITH A PURPOSE
WWW.21STCENTURYPRESS.COM

ACKNOWLEDGEMENT

I would like to express my heartfelt gratitude to my friend, Randy Spencer. His faithful example in ministry, his love and fellowship over the years, and his insight into the Word of God have blessed my life. His selfless service to his congregations, his family, his students and his friends will surely be rewarded when we stand before the throne. Thanks especially for opening my eyes to this beautiful parallel of the staff and the Holy Spirit. May the journey continue.

I would also like to thank my editor, Ruth McClellan for her careful attention to every word and my administrative assistant, Linda Sweat for her usual invaluable support. I couldn't have done it without you.

TABLE OF CONTENTS

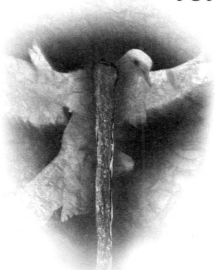

A JOURNEY INTO THE SPIRIT-FILLED LIFE

Rod of the Spirit is a book dealing with a vital issue that will excite and challenge every Christian. This unique study will help you in your desire to live the abundant life that God designed for each of His children. Our God delights in the simple. He often deliberately chooses what the world considers insignificant and foolish to confound those who boast of worldly superiority. God's Word tells us that the Lord uses the weak things of this world to confound the mighty (I Corinthians 1:29-31).

It has often been observed that we tend to overlook the obvious. It is not surprising then that great truth can be found in often-overlooked words, passages, or objects in Scripture. We would do well to look at the significance of an indispensable piece of equipment used by lowly, menial, ancient shepherds. In the obscurity of a simple shepherd's rod, God has concealed valuable lessons to guide us in our sojourn on this earth.

There are striking parallels between the various functions of the Old Testament shepherd's rod and the ever-present ministry of the Holy Spirit in our lives. A careful study of the rod, an object mentioned repeatedly throughout the Bible, reveals that it is a very significant spiritual symbol for the Christian. The ancient rod was not only an implement used by shepherds but was also employed by rulers, teachers, travelers, the physically impaired, and warriors. Our study will examine this common stave, or rod, and its value as it enriches our understanding of the Holy Spirit.

This study of the Old Testament rod sheds new light and provides deeper understanding of the role of the Holy Spirit in the life of the Christian. The Holy Spirit is to have an ever-present ministry in the life of each and every believer. But the sad truth remains that most in the body of Christ know little or nothing of a life lived in the power of the Holy Spirit.

A multitude of books have been written on the subject of Christ revealed in the Old Testament, but one is hard pressed to find much in print on the subject of the symbols of the Holy Spirit in the Old Testament. It is my belief that if every believer became aware of this concept, the symbol of the shepherd's rod would become a familiar emblem, as familiar as the dove, the rainbow, the fish, and the cross. Just as the cross symbolizes the crucified Christ, the shepherd's rod symbolizes the empowering Holy Spirit whose ministry provides comfort, rest, authority, support, power and defense.

My goal in this book is to communicate the dynamic,

Spirit-filled life that should characterize every Christian. This will be done through the study of a simple Biblical object. I hope the book will be a blessing to you as a believer and will reveal the power and presence of a God who dwells in each of us through our Comforter and Helper—the Holy Spirit of the Living God.

THE HOLY SPIRIT REVEALED IN THE ROD

Every book of the Bible contains beautiful types and portrayals of Christ. It has commonly been said that whereas in the Old Testament Christ is concealed, in the New Testament He is revealed. Although many people have studied Christology and are familiar with Old Testament passages relating to Christ, it is not with equal familiarity that they recognize the Person and ministry of the Holy Spirit in the Old Testament.

At first glance, the types and portrayals of the Holy Spirit in the Old Testament books of the law and prophets seem rare and ambiguous. However, upon closer inspection, the ministry and Person of the Holy Spirit are indeed found throughout the Old Testament. This book has been written with the desire that you might gain an understanding of the manifestation and presence of the powerful Holy Spirit. This will be accomplished through the study of an obscure and seemingly insignificant implement known as a rod.

Within the shadow of the primitive rod is revealed God the Holy Spirit, the third Person of the Trinity. True to His very nature and character, He is pictured working unnoticed, offering guidance, powerful assistance, and gentle loving reproof to all who would recognize His presence. The Rod of the Spirit of the New Testament believer is indeed the ever-powerful and ever-present Holy Spirit whom Jesus referred to when He said, "And I will pray the Father, and he shall give you another Comforter, that he may abide with you forever" (John 14:16).

There are many misunderstandings and misconceptions today concerning the ministry of the Holy Spirit. I am convinced that these errors can be resolved if we recognize the lovely portrayals of the Holy Spirit in the Old Testament rod. Even scholars have overlooked the significance of what is described in the Scriptures as a simple shepherd's rod, when in essence it sets forth a wonderful typology of the power and presence of the Holy Spirit and truly foreshadows His future ministry.

The study of the physical uses of the Old Testament rod reveals the nature of the spiritual ministry and working of the Holy Spirit in the New Testament. The rod is mentioned more than 250 times in the Bible. In most instances, it was a physical sign with a much greater spiritual implication. Today, the physical rod which we find in the hands of the Old Testament prophets, has been replaced by the spiritual rod, the Holy Spirit, Who is found in the New Testament. That which God's men once held securely in their hands has today been placed much more securely in our hearts.

Allow me to make one clear distinction before I proceed further on this subject. Since the theme of this book focuses on the indwelling dynamics of the Holy Spirit, it is imperative that I make clear my doctrinal position and then continue to build upon that foundation. According to the Word of God in John 3:3-6, every believer is born of the Spirit: "Jesus answered and said unto him, 'Verily, verily, I say unto thee, Except a man be born again, he cannot see the kingdom of God.' Nicodemus saith unto him, 'How can a man be born when he is old? can he enter the second time into his mother's womb, and be born?' Jesus answered, 'Verily, verily, I say unto thee, except a man be born of water and of the Spirit, he cannot enter into the kingdom of God.'"

First Corinthians 12:13 declares, "For by one Spirit are we all baptized into one body, whether we be Jews or Gentiles; and have been all made to drink into one Spirit." The moment you and I received Jesus Christ as our Lord and Savior, Jesus Christ placed His Spirit into our hearts. We have the Rod of the Spirit, the powerful Holy Spirit indwelling us.

Other verses that confirm that believers receive the Holy Spirit at the time of salvation include: Ephesians 4:4-5, "There is one body, and one Spirit, even as ye are called in one hope of your calling; One Lord, one faith, one baptism." Ephesians 1:13, "In whom ye also trusted, after that ye heard the word of truth, the gospel of your salvation: in whom also, after that ye believed, ye were sealed with that Holy Spirit of promise." Romans 8:9, "But ye are not in the flesh, but in the Spirit, if so be that the Spirit of God dwell in you. Now if any man have not the Spirit of Christ, he is none of his." And Galatians 4:6, "And because ye are sons, God hath sent forth the Spirit of his Son into your hearts, crying, 'Abba, Father.'"

It is very obvious that many Christians are not living in the power of the Spirit. This has nothing to do with receiving the Holy Spirit at the time of salvation. It has everything to do with an irrefutable filling of the Spirit that is an absolute necessity for purity, power, and performance in the work of God. I am referring to a special anointing for holy living and service which I prefer to call "my Rod." Those who live under the control of the Holy Spirit are filled with the truth of Jesus Christ through his Word, and they walk in power as they share the Gospel of Jesus Christ.

One of the most devastating and costly mistakes made by some churches of our day is their conscious denial of the working of the Holy Spirit. During the early days of church history, there was a position taken by some churches that led to the destructive effects known as liberalism. Many churches began to deny the deity of Christ, resulting in their spiritual decay and death. Today many of these mainline denominational churches openly deny the fundamentals of the faith: the virgin birth; the inerrancy, infallibility, and verbal inspiration of the Scriptures; the literal death, burial, and resurrection of Jesus Christ; the new birth experience, and the second coming of Christ. These churches have degenerated into mere social clubs and religious organizations that are empty and void of any spiritual blessings from God.

As a result of their denial of the true ministry of Jesus Christ, Icabod, meaning "the glory of the Lord has departed," could very well be written over their doors. In the same way that liberalism, formalistic orthodoxy, and modernism have removed the blood of Jesus Christ from the salvation experience, many religious institutions have ignored, or even denied, the anointing and convicting power of the Holy Spirit. While one has done a serious injustice to Christ and His work, the other has done an equal disservice to the work of the Holy Spirit. Ponder if you will, the words of one of the spiritual giants of our faith, A.W. Tozier: "If the Lord's people were only half as eager to be filled with the Spirit as they are to prove that you can't be filled with the Spirit, the church would be crowded out."[1]

While some cold, ritualistic, and lethargic churches have no desire to operate in the power of the Spirit of God, there are other churches that desire to follow God but stumble along, never sensing a real move of God in their midst. The preaching is dull and lifeless. Shouts of praise are unheard. The people have not entered into the blessed-ness of Psalm 33:1, "Rejoice in the LORD, O ye righteous: for praise is comely (natural) for the upright." They read Psalm 47:1 with no apparent understanding or practical application, "O chap your hands, all ye people; shout unto God with the voice of triumph." It is no wonder that enthu-siasm for winning the lost for Christ has disappeared, replaced by many busy activities with little meaning.

Many Bible-believing Christians would never admit that they have done an injustice to the personal work of the Holy Spirit. However, the absence of anointing on their min-istries testifies to the fact that something is wrong. This denial has not come by way of an open doctrinal statement but more subtly through reliance on organizational pro-grams, denominational resources, and unbending tradition. Such approaches to ministry have rendered the influence of the Holy Spirit as unnecessary and impractical, negating the need for a victorious daily walk. The dependence upon the

Holy Spirit is so vague that it is nonexistent among many church members. I believe that if God chose today to entirely remove the presence of the Comforter, the Holy Spirit, that ninety percent of all churches would continue to function as though nothing happened. Most Christians would continue with business as usual.

I have a deep desire for every child of God to understand and experience the power and presence of the Holy Spirit of God, which was represented in the Old Testament by the Rod of God. My goal and purpose is that we will walk with the Rod of the Spirit so that we experience the Holy Spirit's filling in our personal lives and that we honor Him and His Lordship in the church of Jesus Christ.

Jesus said in John 4:23-24, "But the hour cometh, and now is, when the true worshippers shall worship the Father in spirit and in truth: for the Father seeketh such to worship him. God is a Spirit: and they that worship him must worship him in spirit and in truth." We see in this passage that the change of worship was from a place to a person. God is a Spirit, and that means that He is not a physical being limited to one place. When you and I worship the Person of the Lord Jesus Christ through the power of the Rod of the Spirit, the Holy Spirit, there will be praise and adoration on our lips and in our life. It is not where we worship that counts but how we worship.

In the presence of an awesome, real God there will be praise, joy, and excitement! People will be saved, and lives will be changed. Scripture tells us that times of refreshing come from the presence of the Lord (Acts 3:19). As God's people come together in a place that is permeated with the Spirit of the Lord, there will be unity, peace, and mighty saving and restoring power. Oh, that many of our churches would get a glimpse of what they are missing!

While those of us who call ourselves fundamentalists take pride in the fact that we hold to the fundamental truths of Scripture, including the Person and work of the Lord Jesus Christ, we often fail to see the fundamental nature of the doctrine of the Holy Spirit and how He was given to work in and through each of us. What a tragedy it would be to live our lives as Christians, knowing that God the Holy Spirit lives within us, yet refusing to allow Him His rightful place of ministry in our lives and in our churches.

You might ask why it is necessary for a believer to prayerfully seek the Holy Spirit when the Spirit has already taken up His residence in the believer at the time of his salvation. God the Holy Spirit lives in the life of every believer, but this does not automatically mean that the believer is allowing the Holy Spirit to control his every thought, word, and deed. It is impossible for anyone to live a godly life without the power of the Holy Spirit. And when a believer's life is godly, it is only natural that you will see a life that is being continually empowered for service.

The Holy Spirit, the third Person of the Divine Godhead, Who is ever present in the heart and life of every blood-bought believer, is directly working in the affairs of men. 1 Corinthians 6:19-20 says, "What! know ye not that your body is the temple of the Holy Ghost which is in you, which ye have of God, and ye are not your own? For ye are bought with a price: therefore glorify God in your body, and in your spirit, which are God's." We are to glorify God by allowing the Holy Spirit to control us so that He might perfect holiness in us by revealing Christ to us. And when our life is pleasing to God because it is controlled by the Holy Spirit, He will use us and infuse us with power that will enable us to build the church of the Lord Jesus Christ.

Have you experienced the Holy Spirit's help? What a comfort it is to know that the Holy Spirit prays for us. Romans 8:26-27 assures us that, "Likewise the Spirit also helpeth our infirmities: for we know not what we should pray for as we ought: but the Spirit itself maketh intercession for us with groanings which cannot be uttered. And he that searcheth the hearts knoweth what is the mind of the Spirit, because he maketh intercession for the saints according to the will of God." Many times I struggle to know how I should pray within the will of God. What a beautiful promise to know that God the Holy Spirit, my ever-present Rod, always prays for me according to the exact will of God!

We know we are loved because of the Holy Spirit's ministry in our lives. In a day and time when more than half of our homes in America are led by a single parent, when abuse is rampant, and dysfunction is becoming the norm, we desperately need to know that we are unconditionally loved by our heavenly Father. Romans 5:5 says, "And hope maketh not ashamed; because the love of God is shed abroad in our hearts by the Holy Ghost which is given unto us."

There is much talk in these tumultuous days about the need for revival in our lives, our homes, our churches, and our nation. It is the Holy Spirit whose convicting power leads to repentance and afterwards gives a deep sense of joy. The lack of these things is an indicator of the lack of supernatural power. We see in Nehemiah 8 that when true revival broke out, the power of God was revealed through tears of repentance, shouts of rejoicing, and commitments to renewal. The Lord knows we need that in our churches today.

What has caused believers to become so insensitive, fearful, and even antagonistic toward the ministry of the Holy Spirit? If there is such a thing as a simple answer to this question, it is probably found in the fear of not wanting to be identified with the wrong group. There is no doubt in my mind that much of what is credited to a moving of the Holy Ghost in many religious circles of our day has done considerable damage because it misrepresents the true ministry of the Spirit of God. This tidal wave of error accompanied by the misinterpretation of Scriptures, fleshly performances, unbiblical practices, indignant behavior, and pandemonium has caused many spiritually-discerning Christians to be wary of anything identified with the name Holy Ghost.

Many church leaders have taken such a strong stand against emotionalism that believers fear any kind of display of feeling or emotion. This fear of emotionalism has reaped the whirlwind of spiritual deadness: no tears, no joyous laughter, no heart-felt shouts or amens, no clapping of the hands, no friendly smiles, no outward expression of feeling, and no spirit.

Sadly, many who have taken issue against the error of emotional exhibitionism have become extremists in the opposite direction. For fear of being labeled "pew jumping, aisle running, holy rollers," they have grieved, quenched, and robbed the Holy Spirit of His true ministry. I think the sense of wonder spoken of in the New Testament and enjoyed by the early Christian church, remains one of God's priorities for every Christian living in this church age.

God has not changed concerning His people. He is the same yesterday, today, and forever (Hebrews 13:8). He longs for believers today to know the joy and expectation felt by the early New Testament church as they saw people saved and added to their numbers daily. These New Testament believers fellowshipped and broke bread together. Because they were controlled by the Holy Spirit, there was great unity among them and love for one another. Church members helped each other and shared their possessions. They experienced the power and blessings of God that extended far beyond their expectations.

The great majority of our churches today seem to have lost the wonder and excitement of the New Testament church. Many no longer seem to seek the presence of an awesome, real God who is mindful to bless us. Psalm 115:12 promises, "The LORD hath been mindful of us: he will bless us." When the Holy Spirit of God permeates and controls the lives of believers and those believers come together as a unified force, the church of the living God will once again know the same miraculous power of the 120 in that upper room. The church will once again be all that God desires it to be. Do you long for the controlling influence of the Holy Spirit in your life and in the life of your church?

Do you have the assurance that what you have experienced in your spiritual life is all that God's promise intended for you when He sent His Spirit to dwell in you? I want to challenge God's people to return to a balanced truth about the Holy Spirit. We need a renewed commitment toward God that is demonstrated through the freedom of the Holy Spirit to direct our every thought, word, and deed. My hope is that you will prayerfully consider these pages with an open mind. My greatest desire and purpose in this writing is to challenge you, as a Christian, to search your heart and sincerely ask yourself, "Have I allowed the Holy Spirit His rightful place in my life and ministry?" I pray that as we consider the shepherd's rod and its striking parallels to the Holy Spirit that we will gain fresh insights into the Person, power, and work of the Holy Spirit of God.

CHAPTER 1

THE POWER OF THE HOLY SPIRIT

Power! The mere mention of the word brings an air of fascination, wonder, and longing. It is probably the most sought after property or distinction on earth, even more so than wealth, fame, or wisdom. Through power all other desires are easily obtained. From the dawn of recorded history, humans have fallen prey to its deception and luring enticements. It was this pursuit of power that led our original parents in the Garden of Eden to disobey God and eat the forbidden fruit. The allure was that they would become like God (Genesis 3:5). Later in time, fallen men made another attempt to achieve a position of power by building a city and a tower whose top reached into heaven (Genesis 11:4). It was Lucifer's quest for power and prestige that led him to rebel against God in his declaration, "I will be like the most High" (Isaiah 14:14).

What is it in the heart of humanity that causes such infatuation with dominance, power, and control? What is the fire that rages in the heart of man, this unquenchable thirst for power? What causes even a small boy to stand in wide-eyed wonder as he gazes at the body builder whose physique ripples with muscles? What is so fascinating about guns like the world-renowned 44 Magnum, the most powerful handgun in the world? Why are movies like *Rambo, Rocky, Commando,* XXX, or any other dozen "tough-guy" movies box-office sellouts? Why is there an innate desire within man to be successful, powerful, and a winner?

Since the beginning of time, political leaders have sought world domination. It is no different today. The ever-increasing quest for power on the world scene is still out of control. The struggle between the world's super-powers continues to rage over the arms race. Could it be that it was Alexander the Great's lust for power that could not be quenched when he cried in desperation, "There are no more worlds to conquer!'

Even the Christian world is vulnerable to man's struggle to attain success. Still fresh in our minds are the memories of the religious media kingdoms that crumbled and became an open reproach to the Christian church. Some church leaders today seem to be in a power struggle to accumulate great wealth and build their own empires. Other well-meaning and sincere preachers of the gospel inwardly war with a spirit of jealousy because they mistakenly compare themselves with others. They lose sight of Christ's teachings on the value of faithfulness above success.

So what is power, and who is the most powerful? Is power in the hands of the one holding the most weapons?

Is strength found in nuclear warheads, ballistic missiles, and megaton bombs? What is more powerful than a cobalt bomb, which in theory can destroy the entire globe if placed at each of the poles and detonated? What is more accurate than the laser beam, that with microscopic precision can etch the entire Lord's Prayer on the head of the pin? What is more complex than the human brain, which can activate millions of brain cells simultaneously? Or what is faster than the spy plane XR71 whose top speed is classified information?

Reality reminds us that there is always someone or something better or more powerful on the horizon. The champion never retains his title. His power is always short-lived and soon surpassed. In his futility to arrive at the zenith of power, man finds that when he has "scratched and clawed" his way to the top, often at an extreme price to himself, his family, and those with whom he has taken advantage, he still has no peace.

It is not until man knows the true Source and Author of power can he understand how power is to be appropriated in his life and world in a way that will bring him fulfillment and joy. Jesus said in Matthew 28:18, "All power is given unto me in heaven and in earth." And then He made this profound promise to believers, "But ye shall receive power, after that the Holy Ghost is come upon you: and ye shall be witnesses unto me both in Jerusalem, and in all Judea, and in Samaria, and unto the uttermost part of the earth" (Acts 1:8). Jesus assigns believers the enormous task of the Great Commission, but He also equips them with a power equal to the task, the power of the Holy Spirit. It is this power that fascinates me and that I long to see manifested in my life.

It was the disciple's presumption that Christ would set

up a powerful earthly kingdom and free them from the rule of their oppressors. Their questions to Christ centered around positions of leadership and authority. While walking with Jesus on the earth, they never fully understood Christ's concept of His ruling the kingdom of their hearts. They were to receive power but not the power of this earth, not the power of position, recognition, fame, wealth, or politics. Their power was to be spiritual and supernatural. It was to be the very power of God Himself, the Supreme Being of the Universe. He would dwell within the heart and life of the believer.

It was not until the Day of Pentecost, when God the Holy Spirit came to indwell them, that the disciples finally understood Christ's teachings. God the Holy Spirit had taken control of them. Experiencing the presence and power of God within their lives was a summit, the supreme experience of their lives. No greater power could ever be possessed by anyone. Nothing else would ever be needed.

Once the disciples experienced the coming of God's Spirit into their lives, they never again asked about earthly power. God's Holy Spirit indwelling a believer is the power of God for which the human heart craves. Once God's Spirit dwells within and controls a person, that person is supremely fulfilled. He has power to live a victorious life. Nothing else can ever satisfy.

After the believers were filled with the Holy Spirit and experienced the power of that filling, that control, they set out to accomplish the task to which they had been commissioned. Each believer is given a task by God, a mission to carry out. It is impossible for man to obey God in his own power. The believer does not have the power to carry out that task. The power of God Himself, the Spirit, is needed.

We have seen how Christ promised power to the believer after he was filled with the Holy Spirit. Both the Spirit of God and His power are promised. It is critical that we as believers understand two great lessons here. As we delineated in Scripture earlier in this book, the Holy Spirit is the Third Person of the Trinity. He is received into the life of a believer at the time of salvation. However, because you possess the Holy Spirit as a believer in the Lord Jesus, does not automatically mean that you are allowing the Holy Spirit to control your life. This accounts for the carnal, unholy lives of most Christians who know little or nothing of what it means to walk in the Spirit. This accounts for the lack of any witness in the lives of most Christians and churches.

Notice that the band of disciples in the upper room were a unified group who were giving themselves to prayer and fasting when the Holy Spirit came. God cannot bless our lives and our work for Him if we are living unholy lives. It is ludicrous to pray for the power of the Holy Spirit to witness if we have refused Him control of all that we are and have. Let us repent of the sin of allowing self, and flesh, and self-will to occupy the place in our hearts that is meant to be occupied every moment by God the Holy Spirit. God blesses the attitude of our hearts. We cannot be holy in ourselves. This is the beauty of the Holy Spirit. When we come to God with a repentant attitude, in humility and utter helplessness, He will fill us and work in us, "For it is God which worketh in you both to will and to do of his good pleasure" (Philippians 2:13).

Many people believe that in order to survive in this world a person must be tough, overbearing, unbending, and harsh. But in a word from the Lord to Zerubbabel, God said, "Not by might, nor by power, but by my spirit, saith the LORD of hosts" (Zechariah 4:6). It is only through God's

Spirit that anything of lasting value is accomplished. As you and I live for God, we must determine not to trust in our own strength or abilities. Instead, we must depend on God to work in the power of His Spirit since it is from Him that we receive our equipping power.

As He did when He was first given, God the Holy Spirit comes upon believers as an *equipping* power. He equips the believer to carry out his task for God, and that task is witnessing. The word witness is not a command; rather it is a natural result of the Holy Spirit's control of the life of a person. It is the same with power. The Word says very simply that a Spirit-filled person has power and becomes a witness for Christ throughout the world. This is important for it makes witnessing and power trademarks of Christian believers. A genuine believer possesses the Spirit Who gives him power, and so he becomes by nature a witness for the Lord.

The hour has come when the Church must exercise a supernatural power. If we are to stand in the last days, it will be through the power of the Spirit. Paul says in Ephesians 6:10, "Finally, my brethren, be strong in the Lord, and in the power of his might." Let us examine the three words, "strong," "power," and "might" that are used to stress the utter necessity of the believer to be strong. The word *strong* (*endunamoo* in Greek) means power, might, and strength. The believer must possess power, might, and strength as he walks through the course of this life. The Lord's *power*, (*kratos*), indicates His Sovereign and unlimited power and dominion over all. The Lord's *might* (*ischuos*) includes strength, force, and ability. This means His ability to use His strength and force wisely, that is, in perfection. The believer is to be mighty in the perfect, Sovereign, and unlimited power of the Lord.

It is vital that we understand and say repeatedly that the believer's strength is not human, fleshly strength. It is not the strength of anything within this world. The believer's strength is found in a living, dynamic relationship with Christ by walking in the Spirit. The Lord is the source of the believer's strength. No other source can give man the strength to overcome this world with all of its trials, temptations, and death.

We give God glory because only He is ". . .able to do exceeding abundantly above all that we ask or think, according to the power that worketh in us" (Ephesians 3:20).

God is able to do what we ask. The word *exceeding* means to surpass, to go beyond any request, to overcome and do anything; *abundantly* means to overflow and do more than enough; *above* means to go over. Imagine going beyond anything that we can think! What is the greatest answer and deliverance of which we can think? God is able to far surpass our feeble imaginings because of His power, the mighty power of the Holy Spirit, working in our lives.

It is this power of the Holy Spirit that gets me excited and that I pray to see evident in my own life and in Christ's churches throughout the world. This is the power that God provided for the church to accomplish its mission. May we be filled with the Spirit of God that He might use our lives to be witnesses throughout the world!

For too long the world has seen the church as weak, anemic, and fragmented. This is because she has been led by men and filled with congregations that are weak, anemic, and fragmented. During these days of uncertainty, the world desperately needs to see a supernatural, God-empowered church that prevails against the onslaught of Satan.

We must remember that Satan is a strong enemy and

that we need the power of God to stand against him. Never underestimate the power of the devil. It is no coincidence that he is compared to a lion and a dragon. The book of Job details what Satan can do to a man's body, home, wealth, and friends. Jesus called Satan a thief who comes to kill, steal, and destroy (John 10:10).

Not only is Satan strong, but he is also wise and subtle. God warns us in Ephesians 6: 11 that we must continually "Put on the whole armor of God, that ye may be able to stand against the wiles of the devil." Wiles refers to cunning, crafty arts, strategy, and tricks. The Christian cannot afford to be ignorant of his methods and devices (II Corinthians 2:11). Some men are cunning and crafty and lie in wait to deceive others (Ephesians 4:14). These men exemplify the deceitful heart of their father Satan who masquerades as an angel of light (II Corinthians 11:14), blinding men's minds to the truth of God's Word.

The Apostle Paul uses the word *wrestle* when he speaks of standing against our enemy. This indicates that we are involved in a hand-to-hand battle and are not mere spectators. Satan wants to use our external enemy, the world, and our internal enemy, the flesh, to defeat us. His weapons and battle plans are very strategically laid out, and that is why it is critical that we be filled with the Holy Spirit and walk in power so that Satan cannot destroy us. Remember I John 4:4, ". . . greater is he that is in you than he that is in the world."

We must continually be reminded that God has called us to live in the power of the Holy Spirit, not in power of the flesh. Our great enemy is the flesh. Paul asked the Galatian Christians, "Are ye so foolish? having begun in the Spirit, are ye now made perfect by the flesh?" We are cautioned in Psalm 127:1, "Except the LORD build the house, they labor in vain that build it: except the LORD keep the city, the watchman waketh but in vain."

Galatians 5:17 warns us that, "The flesh lusteth against the Spirit." The problem is that each of us is fighting an internal war, our flesh versus our Spirit. The flesh is that beachhead of sin where Satan lands to tempt and try us. It is that part of our humanness that exposes our ability to sin. Even though we are new creations and have new natures, we are still human and have the capacity to make wrong choices and sin. The flesh is that element of man that is opposed to goodness, godliness, and righteousness. It is the flesh, the carnal nature that the Apostle Paul refers to in Romans 7:15 when he says, "For that which I do, I allow not: for what I would, that do I not; but what I hate, that do I."

Paul does not leave us in a pitiful condition of sin. He goes on in chapter 7 to record the path to victory in verses 24 and 25, "O wretched man that I am! Who shall deliver me from the body of this death? I thank God through Jesus Christ our Lord!" If you and I will walk continuously controlled by the Spirit of God every moment of every day, conscious of Christ's presence and feeding on His Word, we will not be slaves of the flesh. Two things cannot occupy our minds at the same time. We cannot concentrate on Jesus Christ and temptation at the same time. II Peter 2:9 promises, "The Lord knoweth how to deliver the godly out of temptations, and to reserve the unjust unto the Day of Judgment to be punished."

If we walk controlled by the Spirit, we can have victory over the flesh. It is a tragic fact that Christians can give in to the flesh and sin greatly. Paul lists the works of the flesh in Galatians 5:19-21 as fornication (which is adultery or homosexuality); any sexual sin, uncleanness (which is general impurity of life); lasciviousness (which is sexual perversion); idolatry (which is the worship of idols or anything which takes first place in our lives); sorcery (which also can be interpreted witchcraft and drugs); and then hatred, strife, jealousy, wrath, factions, and seditions (which are revolutions, heresies, envyings, murders, drunkenness, and reveling). These are the characteristics of those who will not inherit the kingdom of God. In other words, this is the way a non-Christian lives.

All the commandments of the New Testament can be reduced to the necessity of walking by the Spirit. Those who walk by the Spirit do not carry out the lusts and desires of the flesh. Our flesh wants to control our actions, thoughts, and feelings. It wants to create anger, hostility, bitterness, jealousy, envy, and strife. It wants us to be fearful, have doubts, and hate God. The flesh is responsible for lives lived in guilt; marriages that are on their way to destruction; children living in rebellion to the ways of God; and unhealthy relationships. Flesh renders us useless to God. The only hope of overcoming the flesh is to walk in the Spirit. Human solutions cannot solve fundamentally spiritual problems. Jesus said, "It is the spirit that quickeneth; the flesh profiteth nothing: the words that I speak unto you, they are spirit, and they are life" (John 6:63).

A Christian may fall into sin, but the conviction of the Holy Spirit will be so strong that he cannot remain there. Galatians 5:18 tells us, "If ye be led of the Spirit, ye are not under the law." Those who do not walk in the Spirit fall under God's law. When that happens, God's law must take its retribution, and the believer falls under God's chastening. "Be sure your sin will find you out" (Numbers 32:23). Galatians 6:7 warns, "Be not deceived; God is not mocked: for whatsoever a man soweth, that shall he also reap." In

His mercy God chastens sin. How thankful I am for His promise in

I Corinthians 11:31, "For if we would judge ourselves, we should not be judged." God delights in showing mercy as evidenced in Proverbs 28:13, "He that covereth his sins shall not prosper: but whoso confesseth and forsaketh them shall have mercy." When a believer sins, he must come before God in brokenness and repent.

Our goal as Christians must be to walk in the Spirit so that we will not fall under the condemnation and consequences of a broken law. Just as Paul lists the works of the flesh, so he lists the fruit that the Spirit produces in a life under His control: "But the fruit of the Spirit is love, joy, peace, long-suffering, gentleness, goodness, faith, meekness, temperance: against such there is no law" (Galatians 5:22, 23). The fruit of the Spirit is the spontaneous work of the Holy Spirit in a believer when he is walking in the Spirit. The Spirit's fruit are Christ's character traits. They are the by-products of His control and cannot be obtained by trying to get them. Only by joining our lives to Christ can we live a life that is pleasing to Christ. We must know Him, love Him, remember Him, and imitate Him. Then we will fulfill the intended purpose of the law of God, to love God and man. Because the God who sent the law also sent the Spirit, the by-products of the Spirit-filled life are in perfect harmony with the intent of God's law. The person who is rich in the fruit of the Spirit actually fulfills the law far better than the legalist.

God's church on this earth is a direct reflection of its leaders and its congregation. As the Holy Spirit is the power of individual believers, He is also the power of the church. It is He Who supervises the work of God on this earth. We cannot expect God to bless our work if we are not doing it under the control of His Spirit to Whom we give proper attention and respect. I have at times encountered preachers who carelessly abuse the power of their position for their own glory or the church's glory. Other times I see churches that do not even seem to notice or care that there is no power in their midst. They have beautiful buildings and sufficient budgets and seem content to go through the motions of church as usual. We can have all the spiritual machinery, but without the oil of the Holy Spirit, the machine will surely fail.

Much is done in our world in the name of religion. Religion is void of the power of the Holy Spirit. In the early days of the New Testament church, the disciples were continually persecuted by the religious leaders of their day who were enraged at their teaching concerning Jesus the Christ. In Acts 4, after the healing of the lame man at the temple gate, Peter and John were brought before the counsel who asked, " By what power, or by what name, have ye done this? " (vs. 7) In Acts 4:8 we read, "Then Peter, filled with the Holy Ghost, said unto them . . ."The actions and words of Peter and John were threatening words to those religious hypocrites who were, for the most part, more interested in their reputations and their position than they were in God. Through the help of the Holy Spirit, Peter spoke boldly before the counsel, actually putting them on trial by showing them their inadequacies and their sins, and presenting them the gospel of Jesus Christ, whom they had crucified but Who had risen again.

I truly believe that many reading this book long, as I do, to know that continual filling of the Holy Spirit. We long to open our mouth, as Peter did, knowing that God the Holy Spirit is directing our words. We long to know that God has commissioned a task particularly for us as He did for Barnabas and Saul when, "As they ministered to the Lord, and fasted, the Holy Ghost said, 'Separate me Barnabas and Saul for the work whereunto I have called them.'" (Acts 13:3).

Before we can speak for God and do the work He has specifically designed for us to do, we must live for God. Does the Holy Spirit still fill men and women today so that their lives are characterized by love, joy, peace, longsuffering, gentleness, goodness, faith, meekness, and self-control? Does the Holy Spirit still direct believers today? Does He still fill their mouths with bold words that bear a powerful witness? He most certainly does! God would not give us a command that is impossible to carry out, "And be not drunk with wine, wherein is excess; but be filled with the Spirit; speaking to yourselves in psalms and hymns and spiritual songs, singing and making melody in your heart to the Lord; giving thanks always for all things unto God and the Father in the name of our Lord Jesus Christ" (Ephesians 5:18-20).

God's desire for His children is that they be controlled by the Holy Spirit continuously. To some this seems very foreign. The problem is not with Him; it is with us. Many are living anemic, powerless Christian lives because they have no idea what it means to be controlled by the Holy Spirit. Others work diligently and sacrificially for God in their own strength, knowing little power or fulfillment. God cannot fill us with His Holy Spirit until we are empty. As we progress in this book we will see many ways in which God works to empty us so that He can fill us. God will meet you at the point of your need. How desperate are you to know the filling of the Holy Spirit? Perhaps you have been discouraged in your Christian walk due to lack of discipline or consistency, but you long to know the filling of the Holy

Spirit as a daily experience. You long to be controlled by the Holy Spirit moment by moment and to manifest the fruit of the Spirit. Be assured that God will bless the longing of your heart and begin His work in you.

Let us today make a renewed commitment to consistent and diligent study of the Word of God. Only then can we know the mind of the Spirit. Let us also make a renewed commitment to fervent and consistent prayer. Only then can we know the will of the Spirit. As we continue our study, ask God to reveal to you the truth about the infilling of His blessed Holy Spirit as you study the Word. Colossians 3:16 instructs us to, "Let the word of Christ dwell in you richly in all wisdom." If we are faithful to study the Word daily, God's Word will dominate our thinking, and our thinking will dominate our actions. The Lord tell us in Proverbs, "For as he thinketh in his heart, so is he" (23:7). "Keep thy heart with all diligence; for out of it are the issues of life" (4:23).

As the Word moves through our hearts and minds when we think and meditate upon its wisdom, the Spirit of God will correct our lives. It is critically important that we spend time in the Word and in prayer, communing with the living God and building an intimate relationship with Him. We have God's promise that, "The steps of a good man are ordered by the LORD: and he delighteth in his way" (Psalm. 37:23). The Bible does not teach the eradication of sin in this life; nor does it teach a second work of grace whereby a person becomes perfect and never sins again. But it does promise a life of victory and fulfillment as we allow the Holy Spirit to control our lives. The spiritual walk is accomplished moment by moment as we die to self and walk by the Spirit. It depends on our submissive yieldedness to the authority of the leadership of the Holy Spirit through the Word of God and constant, intense prayer.

Let us stop at this point and look over the last few years of our lives and ask ourselves this question: Am I walking in the Spirit? Is there continual growth in Christ evidenced in my life? Am I getting better in my thought life, my attitudes, and my actions? Although change can be slow, it will only come as we walk in the Spirit. I appreciate this little verse: "You are writing a gospel, a chapter each day, by the deeds that you do and the words that you say. Men read what you write distorted or true. What is the gospel according to you?" We are to, "Walk as children of light" (Ephesians 5:8) because our actions reflect our faith. In these last days before Jesus returns for His church, let us, "See then that ye walk circumspectly, not as fools, but as wise, redeeming the time, because the days are evil" (Ephesians 5:15,16).

CHAPTER 2

THE ANCIENT ROD

We live in the age of jets, ocean liners, space shuttles, buses, trains, and automobiles. In a matter of hours, a person can travel anywhere in the world with hardly taking a step. In today's era of rapid travel, discussion concerning an ancient, rather obscure and primitive rod or stick seems somewhat odd. Its use as a walking stick seems obsolete and of little need. In the place of bunions and blisters, we get jet lag. One would be hard pressed in America to find a shepherd with a rod staying in a field keeping watch over his flocks. Is it any wonder that most of us have never seen a genuine shepherd's rod? To be quite frank, no one probably really cares to see one. Asked to describe what a rod is, we would have to draw from what we were told as children in Sunday school or from what we have seen in Bible picture books or in a Bible drama on television. Although the rod seems as old as Moses and as lost as sheep in a wilderness, it still has great significance for us today.

I would like to propose that the simple shepherd's rod of Biblical days has a powerful message for us today as we search for the fullness of the Holy Spirit in our lives. I challenge you to examine with me the precious Holy Spirit of God who is the ultimate source of spiritual power, far surpassing man's intelligence and technological prowess. As we study the striking parallels between the Old Testament rod and the Holy Spirit, we will be enriched and enlightened. Because the rod is so unfamiliar and foreign to most of us, allow me to dig it up, dust it off, and introduce you to this priceless tool. I believe it would be wise for every Christian to understand the significance of the rod and the power that it represents.

I have discovered the rod's deep spiritual significance displayed throughout the Old Testament. My study has shown that the rod is mentioned over 250 times in the Holy Scriptures. Let us turn our attention to some of those references that reveal the true meaning of the rod. The Hebrew word *metteh* is translated as *rod, staff, shaft,* or *branch*. The basic meaning of *metteh* is *staff*. The Greek word *rhabdos*, which is the Septuagint rendering of *metteh*, can also be translated *staff* or *staves*, which simply means a sharp pointed stick. The same Greek word is used for *rod* and signifies a piece of tree limb used as a support or a weapon.

As I searched deeper into the Scriptures, I found even more uses of this ancient and very familiar piece of equipment. Jacob used the rod or staff to change the color of Laban's goats and sheep (Genesis 30:36-41). The rod was used as a symbol of authority or as a scepter (Hebrews 1:8). Men and animals were disciplined or smote with the rod (Exodus 21:20, Numbers 22:27, and I Samuel 17:40). We can infer that grain was sometimes beaten out with a rod (Judges 6:11 and Ruth 2:17). The rod was used by the people for support or defense (Exodus 21:19 and Zechariah 8:4). It was also used by travelers as walking sticks (Genesis 32:10, Exodus 12:11, and Matthew 10:10).

Each of the physical functions of the rod or staff includes beautiful implications, symbols, emblems, and ties to the Holy Spirit that unfolds into spiritual application. It is quite interesting how the two words *metteh* and *rhabdos* are used in the Scriptures. I found that a striking parallel can be drawn between the use of the rod in ancient times to the present day ministry of the Holy Spirit. I believe that in many references to the rod throughout the Old and New Testaments there are parallels of the Holy Spirit which carry implications for us as believers and have generally gone overlooked in past studies.

One of the first uses of the rod is found in Genesis 38 when Judah the shepherd gave his rod to his daughter-in-law Tamar. The rod was left with Tamar as a surety that he would keep his promise and return with a kid from the flock. Verse 18 reads, "And he said, 'What pledge shall I give thee?' and she said, 'Thy signet and thy bracelet and thy staff that is in thy hand.'" Likewise, we Christians have a promise from the Lord that he will return just as He promised (Joel 2:28-29, Zechariah 12:10, and John 14:16).

In the sanctification process, the Holy Spirit secures every believer's eternal inheritance. Ephesians 1:13-14 says, "In whom ye also trusted, after that ye heard the word of truth, the gospel of your salvation: in whom also, after that ye believed, ye were sealed with that Holy Spirit of promise, who is the earnest (guarantee) of our inheritance until the redemption of the purchased possession, unto the praise of his glory." The Greek word translated "sealed" here speaks of authenticity and unbreakable promise. The Holy Spirit secures us for all eternity. The Greek word translated "pledged," *arrabon*, speaks of a down payment made to secure a purchase. The moment you and I were saved, the Holy Spirit became our down payment on God's final installment for our eternal glory. In Modern Greek, *arrbon*, with the long vowel mark over "o," includes the idea of an engagement ring. In that sense we can view the Holy Spirit as God's engagement ring, a sign of His deep love and His guarantee to keep His promises.

You may ask, "What about Judas? Was he secure? How did he fall? Why did Jesus not keep him safe?" Judas was never one of Christ's own. Jesus faithfully kept all that the Father gave to Him. Judas was not a believer (John 6:64-71). He had never been cleansed (John 13:11). He had not been among the chosen (John 13:18). He had never been given to Christ (John 18:8-9). Judas is not an example of a believer who lost his salvation; he is an example of an unbeliever who pretended to have salvation but was finally exposed as a fraud. Jesus keeps all that the Father gives to Him (John 10:26-30). We are over-comers because we share His light and have the Rod of the Spirit who seals us.

Let us look at the rod as a symbol of authority. God gave Assyria His staff, a rod as He commissioned Assyria to go in God's power and carry His sword into battle. Isaiah 10:5-6 says, "O Assyrian, the rod of mine anger, and the staff in their hand is mine indignation. I will send him against an hypocritical nation, and against the people of my wrath will I give him a charge, to take the spoil, and to take the prey, and to tread them down like the mire of the streets." Also, in the Psalms and in the books of the Prophets it is repeatedly mentioned that when God sets up His Messianic Kingdom during the Millennium, He will rule with a strong rod or staff. "The Lord shall send the rod of thy strength out of Zion" (Psalm 110:2).

Our spiritual scepter today is the Holy Spirit. Before He ascended to the Father after His resurrection, Jesus gave his disciples the Great Commission for carrying out His work upon the earth. He knew they had no power within themselves to carry out such a great command. That is why He gave the promise in Acts1:8. Not only do we need the Spirit's power to do God's work, we need Christ's mind. Jesus has definite plans with regard to his Kingdom. Only as we are led by the Holy Spirit can we clearly and rightly fit into those plans. A lost world desperately depends on us to know the mind of Christ through our Rod.

The rod was an ancient means of defense. The Bible says, "Thou didst strike through with his staves the head of his villages: they came out as a whirlwind to scatter me" (Habakkuk 3:14). As Christians, we know that our warfare is not physical but spiritual. Ephesians 6:12 declares, "For we wrestle not against flesh and blood, but against principalities, against powers, against the rulers of the darkness of this world, against spiritual wickedness in high places." This verse reveals that the forces of evil that stand against the believer are powerful and large in number. They are apparently organized into a government or hierarchy of evil. These principalities, powers, and rulers of this world in high places all point to a ranking of spiritual forces with enormous authority, position, and rule. Also the forces of evil are the rulers of the darkness of this world.

Darkness in the Bible means the ignorance of truth. It is the opposite of the true nature and purpose of things. For example, what is the source of man and his world? What is man's purpose? What is the end of man and his world? Is there life after earthly existence ceases? Darkness is not knowing these things. It is being ignorant of them. *Light* is knowing God and His Son, Jesus Christ and being filled with the Holy Spirit of God. God the Father, God the Son, and God the Holy Spirit, stand as the source, the purpose, and the end of man and his world.

The Old Testament rod or staff was a means of demonstrating power and was used in performing miracles. Aaron's rod budded to authenticate his priesthood. Moses' rod turned into a serpent and swallowed the serpent-rod of James and Jambre. The Egyptian magicians used staffs as symbols of the powers of the magical realm by which they counterfeited Moses' miracles (Exodus 7:12). We know that genuine miracles only come from the Spirit of God.

We find the rod being used as a prodding stick to guide and move herds in certain directions. Men and women, as well as animals, were goaded by the staff or rod (Exodus 21:20, Numbers 22:27, and I Samuel 17:43). Sharp stabs or pricks of the rod were used on many occasions to bring correction and guidance to the flock to keep them from straying. Thus, the Holy Spirit pricks our hearts today and uses the sharp stabs of conviction to direct us to Christ. After Peter concluded his powerful, Spirit-anointed sermon on the Day of Pentecost, Scripture tells us that the people ". . . were pricked in their heart, and said unto Peter and to the rest of the apostles, 'Men and brethren, what shall we do?'" The people were deeply moved and cried out in conviction. The plain word of Peter's sermon was driven home to their hearts through the power of the Holy Spirit of God.

The word *pricked* is the Greek word *kapenugesan*, which means to convict, stain, sense pain and hurt. Conviction is an emotional movement of the heart. It is a person's acknowledgement of and sorrow for having sinned against God. Godly sorrow results in repentance and brokenness. Conviction leads to a sense of needing more of the Lord and His righteousness. It causes people to seek answers and to ask, "What shall we do?" This is one of the purposes of the power of the Holy Spirit of God in our lives. "And when he [the Holy Spirit] is come, he will reprove [convict] the world of sin, and of righteousness, and of judgment" (John 16:8). It is the Holy Spirit's function to convict the world of its curse, which is sin; its cure, which is righteousness; and its condemnation, which is judgment.

Thus far we have seen the staff being used by rulers, warriors, magicians, and farmers. Let us further note the use of the rod as a teacher. II Samuel 7:14 reads, "I will be his father, and he shall be my son. If he commit iniquity, I will chasten him with the rod of men, and with the stripes of the children of men." On numerous occasions Proverbs mentions the use of the rod in child training or discipline: "He that spareth his rod hateth his son: but he that loveth him chasteneth him betimes" (13:24); and "The rod and reproof give wisdom: but a child left to himself bringeth his mother to shame" (29:15). The staff was used to give direction or training to the child or student. The basic use of the rod was not necessarily for physical correction but rather for instruction and direction.

Christians have the Word of God and the Holy Spirit within them to be their guides to help them test questionable teachings and to make sure they have been instructed in the right way. To stay true to Christ, we must follow His Word and His Spirit, which discern truth from error. I John 2:27 confirms, "But the anointing which ye have received of him abideth in you, and ye need not that any man teach you: but as the same anointing teacheth you of all things, and is truth, and is no lie, and even as it hath taught you, ye shall abide in him."

The Holy Spirit is called the Spirit of truth. He speaks only the truth and guides believers into all truth. The truth, of course, is Jesus Christ Himself. The Spirit leads the believer to Christ, the Truth, and teaches him all the truth about Christ. Jesus said, "But when the Comforter is come, whom I will send unto you from the Father, even the Spirit of truth, which proceedeth from the Father, he shall testify of me" (John 15:26).

It is important to note that the Comforter comes only from the Father in the name of Jesus. In calling God "Father," the father-child relationship is stressed. We must become a child of God, that is, of the Father, in order to be given the Father's comfort. The words "in the name of Jesus" mean that one must approach the Father in the name of Christ. That is recognizing that Jesus alone is acceptable to God. The purpose of the Holy Spirit in the believer's life is two-fold. The first is to teach all things. The Holy Spirit teaches us, not only through the words, but also through the life of Christ. We have the theory as well as the practice, both the principles and the conduct, both the morality and the behavior.

In John 14:26 we see that Christ promised to send the Holy Spirit to teach his followers and to remind them of all that He had taught them: "But the Comforter, which is the Holy Ghost, whom the Father will send in my name, he shall teach you all things, and bring all things to your remembrance, whatsoever I have said unto you." This promise ensures the validity of the New Testament. The disciples were eyewitnesses of Jesus' life and teachings, and the Holy Spirit helped them remember without taking away their individual perspectives. We can be confident that the gospels are accurate records of what Jesus lived and taught.

One of the purposes of the Holy Spirit in the life of the believer is to help him remember all that he has been taught in the Word of God. This is especially important in moments of trial when the truth is needed. The Holy Spirit either infuses the believer with the strength to endure or flashes across his mind the way to escape in accordance with I Corinthians 10:13, "There hath no temptation taken you but such as is common to man: but God is faithful, who will not suffer you to be tempted above that ye are able; but will with the temptation also make a way to escape, that ye may be able to bear it." In John 16:13 we read, "Howbeit when he, the Spirit of truth, is come, he will guide you into all truth: for he shall not speak of himself; but whatsoever he shall hear, that shall he speak: and he will show you things to come."

We must realize that God's wisdom is revealed only by God's Spirit. Paul freely acknowledged this in I Corinthians 3:13, "Which things also we speak, not in the words which man's wisdom teacheth, but which the Holy Ghost teacheth; comparing spiritual things with spiritual." Human reason can never discover God and the things of God. No person knows what is really going on in a man except the man's spirit. So it is with God. No man really knows the things of God except the Spirit of God. Therefore, the world does not know God and the things of God, for they must be revealed. Man cannot enter into the spiritual world on his own. No person has ever seen God. No matter what some people might claim, if we are to ever know the spiritual world and the dimensions of being, God has to reveal Himself. This He did once for all in Christ Jesus, His only beloved Son. Only the man who receives Christ and is born again by the Spirit of God is quickened to understand spiritual things.

The Holy Spirit guides believers by speaking the truth of the Word of God. Christ said that He had many things to say to the apostles that they were not able to bear. "I have yet many things to say unto you, but ye cannot bear them now" (John 16:12). That word, *bear*, literally means to handle or grasp. Christ tells the Spirit what to say and how to guide believers. Jesus knows the infirmities and needs of man through personal experience (Hebrews 4:15, 16). Therefore, He is the one who is appointed by God to instruct the Spirit in His guiding ministry. This truth should cause our hearts to leap with unbelievable joy, confidence, and boldness!

The Lord knows exactly what we face, and He knows exactly what we need! He has given us God the Holy Spirit to live within us and guide us. Rest in the comfort of these great promises: "For as many as are led by the Spirit of God, they are the sons of God" (Romans 8:14). "For this God is our God forever and ever: he will be our guide even unto death" (Psalm 48:14). "Thou shalt guide me with thy counsel [that is the Word of God], and afterward receive me to glory" (Psalm 73:24). "And thine ears shall hear a word behind thee, saying, 'This is the way, walk ye in it, when ye turn to the right hand, and when ye turn to the left'" (Isaiah 30:21). "And I will bring the blind by a way that they knew not; I will lead them in paths that they have not known: I will make darkness light before them, and crooked things straight. These things will I do unto them, and not forsake them" (Isaiah 42:16).

The Holy Spirit guides by showing, announcing, and declaring things to come. After Jesus arose from the dead, the Holy Spirit led the apostles to write the New Testament and to foresee the things revealed in those pages. The Holy Spirit shows, declares, and announces the Word of God to the heart of the believer. This happens when the filling and anointing is prevalent in our lives. "Now we have received, not the spirit of the world, but the Spirit which is of God; that we might know the things that are freely given to us of God" (I Corinthians 2:12). As believers, we must be dependent upon the Holy Spirit's leadership in learning and in walking in the truth. Our growth is progressive, coming only as the Holy Spirit opens up the Word to us.

We see that the rod is found in the hand of every person facing the adversities of life. Those who have been beset by the world use it to give themselves support and rest, as seen in Exodus 21 which deals with the judgments of the law for personal injuries caused to others. Verse 19, which deals specifically with the punishment given to one who smote another and caused injury, reads, "If he rise again, and walk abroad upon his staff, then shall he that smote him be quit: only he shall pay for the loss of his time, and shall cause him to be thoroughly healed." According to the Law, if a man smote or hit another and he died, that man should also be put to death. But if the one smitten were crippled and could move about upon his staff or rod, then restitution was made for his lost wages. The point I wish to make is simply this: those injured in life used the staff or rod as an aid of recovery to support them in their continued endeavors.

In the New Testament, the church was hampered through persecution as recorded in the book of Acts. The Holy Spirit ministered as a comforter and a helper, enabling the church to triumph. Acts 9:31 states, "Then had the churches rest throughout all Judaea and Galilee and Samaria, and were edified; and walking in the fear of the Lord, and in the comfort of the Holy Ghost, were multiplied." Therefore, we see the Holy Spirit is a believer's spiritual support when he is maimed in the spiritual warfare of life.

The rod was found in the hand of every traveler to assist

him as a simple walking stick. As Jacob traveled he said, "... for with my staff I passed over this Jordan" Genesis 32:10. Likewise, the Holy Spirit becomes a walking stick for every believer or pilgrim. We are pilgrims, sojourners on this earth, passing through on our way to eternity. Just as Jesus Christ is the primary Person behind justification, the Holy Spirit is the primary Person behind sanctification. A believer can no more sanctify himself than he could have saved himself in the first place. He cannot live the Christian life by his own resources any more than he could have saved himself by his own resources. We can accomplish our temporary stay on this earth victoriously only as we walk under the power and direction of the Holy Spirit (Galatians 5:16-25 and Romans 8:1).

The rod was carried by everyone from the youngest to the oldest. It was certainly a very common item in ancient Jerusalem. Zechariah 8:4 says, "Thus sayeth the LORD of hosts; there shall yet old men and old women dwell in the streets of Jerusalem, and every man with his staff in his hand for every age." It was just as common to see people holding a rod or a staff in Old Testament times, as it is to see people wearing shoes today. The Christian is personally indwelt by the Holy Spirit, and every believer has the promise of His presence. Every blood-bought believer is a temple for Him to dwell in His fullness. I do not have just a part or portion of the Holy Spirit but rather enjoy and claim Him wholly as mine.

I hope by now it is obvious to every reader that the rod was more than a mere shepherd's tool. We have seen the rod in the hands of rulers, magicians, farmers, travelers, and the common man. It was, without a doubt, a very familiar instrument to all and had many different uses. However, I do not intend to neglect the most important use of the rod as the shepherd's tool. I hope it will become clear that the rod is an emblem of the Holy Spirit foreshadowing His work in the life of each believer.

The rod was a long stick with a crook or hook on the top that was an indispensable piece of equipment to shepherds of old. It was an aid in climbing hills, beating down the brush, driving off beasts of prey, and directing stray sheep. Every shepherd took special pride in the selection of a rod that was just right for him, one exactly suited to his size, strength, and personal use. Since he could only carry the barest of essentials, it was his most prized possession. It was a precious comfort to the shepherd as he leaned on it for support.

The word *comfort* is the very word that Jesus used to describe the Holy Spirit. Note John 14:27, "Peace I leave with you, my peace I give unto you: not as the world giveth, give I unto you. Let not your heart be troubled, neither let it be afraid." The result of the Holy Spirit's working in our lives is a deep lasting peace, unlike worldly peace, which is usually defined as "the absence of conflict." This peace is confident assurance in any circumstance. With Christ's peace, we have no need to fear anything. If our lives are full of stress, we must allow the Holy Spirit to fill us. If our lives are full of problems, we must not worry because the Holy Spirit will see us through. "Be careful for nothing; but in every thing by prayer and supplication with thanksgiving let your requests be made known unto God. And the peace of God, which passeth all understanding, shall keep your hearts and minds through Christ Jesus" (Philippians 4:6-7). Jesus places into the hand of every believer a comforting Rod Who offers sweetness, consolation, and a gentle loving relationship. Through the Holy Spirit, His Rod, Jesus shepherds us every day of our lives.

Generally speaking, we know very little about shepherding. Upon studying shepherds, I learned that the rod was used for three significant roles. We will conclude this chapter by reviewing these roles that have previously been mentioned. Please allow me to quote from Philip Keller's book; A *Shepherd Looks at Psalm 23*. Philip Keller is equipped with a shepherd's experience and personal insight, and he clearly describes the three areas of sheep management in which the rod plays a significant role:

> The first of these lies in drawing sheep together into an intimate relationship. The shepherd will use his staff to gently lift a newborn lamb and bring it to its mother if they become separated. He does this because he does not wish to have the ewe reject her offspring if it bears the odor of his hands upon it. I have watched skilled shepherds moving swiftly with their staffs amongst thousands of ewes that were lambing simultaneously. With deft but gentle strokes the newborn lambs are lifted with the staff and placed side by side with their dams. It is a touching sight that can hold one spellbound for hours.

> But in precisely the same way, the staff is used by the shepherd to reach out and catch individual sheep, young or old, and draw them close to himself for intimate examination. The staff is very useful this way for the shy and timid sheep that normally tend to keep at a distance from the shepherd.

The staff is also used for guiding sheep. Again and again I have seen a shepherd use his staff to guide his sheep gently into a new path or through some gate or along dangerous, difficult routes. He does not use it actually to beat the beast. Rather, the tip of the long slender stick is laid gently against the animal's side and the pressure applied guides the sheep in the way the owner wants it to go. Thus the sheep is reassured of its proper path.

Another common occurrence was to find sheep stuck fast in labyrinths of wild roses or brambles where they had pushed in to find a few stray mouthfuls of green grass. Soon the thorns were so hooked in their wool they could not possibly pull free, tug as they might. Only the use of a staff could free them from their entanglement."[1]

This excerpt is a beautiful portrait depicting the gentle use of the shepherd's rod; spiritual implications concerning the rod are even more fascinating and beautiful. We were once lost sheep, sought out by a loving Shepherd Who used the rod of His Spirit to draw us into an intimate relationship. Just as the shepherd loves the lambs and does not want to see them rejected, so our Shepherd loves each of us and longs for us to be united with Him through the drawing power of the Rod, the Holy Spirit. Isaiah tells us, "All we like sheep have gone astray; we have turned every one to his own way; and the LORD hath laid on him the iniquity of us all" (53:6). John shows us that; "No man can come to me, except the Father which hath sent me draw him" (6:44). God, not man, plays the most active role in salvation. When you and I chose to believe in Jesus Christ as Lord and Savior, we did so only in response to the urging and the power of the Holy Spirit. The Lord does the urging; then we decide whether or not to believe.

The shepherd used the rod to guide his sheep along the proper paths to green pastures and still waters. Gently, but with necessary pressure, he led them in the way that they should go. Our call and promise as believers is, "O come, let us worship and bow down: let us kneel before the LORD our maker. For he is our God; and we are the people of his pasture, and the sheep of his hand" (Psalm 95: 6-7). Just as sheep trust their shepherd, we too can rest in and trust our loving Shepherd Who will guide us in His ways until the day He takes us home. "Know ye that the LORD he is God: it is he that hath made us, and not we ourselves; we are his people, and the sheep of his pasture" (Psalm 100:3).

Finally, the shepherd used His rod to rescue the sheep. They would inevitably get entangled in the brambles of life. As hard as they tried, they could not untangle themselves. The shepherd would search for them until He found them. Only his staff could free them. God knows that we are frail humanity. He knew would need a Helper to come alongside us, and a Comforter to lift us up. God the Holy Spirit, our Rod, rescues and preserves us.

In summary, it is absolutely crucial that we as believers know the control of the Rod of the Spirit in our daily lives. When we became Christians, God's Spirit convicted us of our sins, brought us to repentance, and then regenerated us. He indwelt, baptized, sealed, gifted, and separated us from sin. In the on-going process of sanctification, He gives us access to God, Who supplies all the resources we

need for physical and spiritual life. We are not left to floun-
der, seeking solutions to spiritual needs on the natural
plane. The Spirit illuminates our understanding of God's
Word so that we are transformed by its principles as He
applies them to our lives.

It is our responsibility to be filled with the Spirit and to
walk in the Spirit each day. It is necessary to be reminded of
these basics truths because we often forget the source of
our spiritual power. If your desire is to live a godly life, you
must move into the presence of God through prayer and
allow His Spirit to minister to you and transform you
through His Word. It is my earnest prayer that you will, as
you study this book, know the control of the Rod of the
Spirit, the blessed Holy Spirit, in a new way that will revo-
lutionize your life and ministry. He promises to fill the
heart that is humble, empty of self, and desperate for Him.

CHAPTER 3

THE SPIRIT'S ROD FOR THE JOURNEY

You and I have been put on this earth to fulfill a journey assigned to us by our God. Only He knows the length of our pilgrimage, what twists and turns we will encounter in the way, and when our passage will end. What we do know is that He has promised to be with us every moment and step of the way, living within us and guiding us through the precious Holy Spirit He has given to each of us as believers. He comforts us with the knowledge that this earth is not our home; we are sojourners, passing through on our way to eternity. Our citizenship is in heaven, and as foreigners, He warns us not to love the world or its contents (I John 2:15). We are not earthly beings who are spiritual. Rather, we are spiritual beings who must live on this earth for a short time.

When the disciples walked this earth with Christ Jesus,

55

they did not have the advantage you and I have as believers today. They did not have the completed cannon of Scripture to instruct them or the Holy Spirit living within them to teach them. They clung to Jesus and misunderstood much of what He tried to teach them about Himself and about One He called the Comforter.

As the intimacy of the cross drew near, Jesus knew that His earthly ministry would soon end. He would no longer be with the disciples in bodily form. They had not yet fully comprehended the fact that Jesus would, in order to fulfill the Old Testament Scriptures, soon be put to death and that their lives would be greatly changed. These twelve men had left all to follow Jesus—their jobs, their homes, their friends, and their personal ambitions in life. They had become totally dependent upon Him as the One who had provided for their every spiritual, physical, emotional, and material need. When they needed food, He had multiplied the loaves and the fishes. When Peter needed money for the temple tax, Jesus had supplied that need by means of a coin found in the mouth of a fish. When the disciples needed protection, He had rescued them from every perilous and dangerous situation. In every circumstance, their needs had been surely and securely provided for by the Lord Himself. They knew through experience what Paul wrote about in Philippians 4:19, "But my God shall supply all your need according to His riches in glory by Christ Jesus." The disciples had spent much time alone with the Master. They had sat at His feet, listened to His teachings, and saw His miracles.

When Jesus knew that His departure was drawing near, He was concerned that the disciples learn dependence upon the Holy Spirit who would descend from heaven following His ascension. This truth is seen in John 14:16-19, where

Jesus said, "And I will pray the Father, and he shall give you another Comforter, that he may abide with you forever; Even the Spirit of truth; whom the world cannot receive, because it seeth him not, neither knoweth him: but ye know him; for he dwelleth with you, and shall be in you. I will not leave you comfortless: I will come to you. Yet a little while, and the world seeth me no more; but ye see me: because I live, ye shall live also." Jesus was preparing the hearts of the disciples for the descent of the Holy Spirit who would take His place in His earthly ministry.

The descent of the Holy Spirit marked a major transition in the lives of the disciples and subsequently in the lives of all believers from that time on. In the Old Testament we find spiritual nurturing by God the Father. In the New Testament, we see the physical embrace of Jesus during His earthly ministry. The disciples were on the brink of experiencing the sustaining ministry provided by the Third Person of the Trinity, the Holy Spirit. This sustaining ministry would continue throughout the duration of the Church Age. The disciples had to learn quickly that Jesus would no longer walk with them in His physical form. They needed to learn to depend upon another power.

In the preceding verses in John 14, we see that Jesus told His disciples that the Holy Spirit would never leave them; the world at large could not recognize the Holy Spirit; and God the Holy Spirit would live within them. Jesus also taught the disciples that the Holy Spirit would teach them and remind them of Jesus' words (John 14:26, 15:26). He would reprove the world of sin, show God's righteousness, and announce God's judgment on evil (John 16:8). The Holy Spirit would guide them into truth and give them insight into future events (John 16:13). He would always glorify Christ (John 16:14).

The Holy Spirit has been active from the beginning of time, but after Pentecost in Acts 2 He came to live in all believers. Many people are unaware of the Holy Spirit's activities, but those who receive Christ's words and the Holy Spirit's power experience the abiding, powerful presence of the Holy Spirit. When Jesus said, "I will come to you," (John 14:18) He meant exactly that. Although Jesus ascended to heaven, He sent the Holy Spirit to live in believers; to have the Holy Spirit is to have Jesus Himself. The word translated *comforter* combines the meaning of "comfort" and "counsel." The Holy Spirit is a powerful Person on our side working for us, with us, and in us.

In order to teach this very important lesson to His disciples, Jesus brought an unusual set of circumstances into their lives. This is seen in Mark 6: 7-13:

> "And he called unto him the twelve, and began to send them forth by two and two; and gave them power over unclean spirits; And commanded them that they should take nothing for their journey, save a staff only; no scrip, no bread, no money in their purse: But be shod with sandals; and not put on two coats. And he said unto them, In what place soever ye enter into an house, there abide till ye depart from that place. And whosoever shall not receive you, nor hear you, when ye depart thence, shake off the dust under your feet for a testimony against them. Verily I say unto you, It shall be more tolerable for Sodom and Gomorrha in the day of judgment, than for that city. And they went out, and preached that men should repent. And they cast out many devils, and

anointed with oil many that were sick, and
healed them."

Particularly note verse 8, "And commanded them that
they should take nothing for their journey, save a staff
only." They were told to take nothing for their journey
except a staff or rod. Like every passage of Scripture, this
passage is given for a specific reason. We know that
because II Timothy 3:16,17 tell us, "All Scripture is given by
inspiration of God, and is profitable for doctrine, for
reproof, for correction, for instruction in righteousness:
That the man of God may be perfect, thoroughly furnished
unto all good works." Wherein lies the reason for this particular portion of Scripture? In order to better understand
the specific instructions given to the twelve disciples in
Mark 6, we will cautiously proceed through these verses to
discover what valuable insights the Holy Spirit wishes to
reveal.

In light of the context, let us look at the commission
given. Jesus calls His disciples together and issues the commission found in Mark 6:7. He sends them out two by two
with power over unclean spirits. They were about to
embark on their first solo flight. The disciples had been
taught by Jesus, and now they must teach others His
gospel. They were sent forth on a missionary journey. This
is the beginning of the church planting age. The commission was the same as that of believers today. We are commanded of God to go into all the world and preach the
gospel to every creature (Mark 16:15). The burden of the
Great Commission still weighs heavily on the shoulders of
every believer. In Matthew 28:18-20 Jesus said, "All power is
given unto me in heaven and in earth. Go ye therefore, and
teach all nations, baptizing them in the name of the Father,

and of the Son, and of the Holy Ghost: Teaching them to observe all things whatsoever I have commanded you: and, lo, I am with you always, even unto the end of the world." Do you see in the latter part of the verse the specific promise of Jesus to go with us? How can He accompany us if He is no longer present on the earth? He uses His agent, the Holy Spirit.

Continuing in Mark 16:15-18, further instructions of this commission are given to us as Christ's followers. He said to them:

> "Go ye into all the world, and preach the gospel to every creature. He that believeth and is baptized shall be saved; but he that believeth not shall be damned. And these signs shall follow them that believe; In my name shall they cast out devils; they shall speak with new tongues; They shall take up serpents; and if they drink any deadly thing, it shall not hurt them; they shall lay hands on the sick, and they shall recover."

The disciples were given specific orders to go among the heathen, as lambs among wolves, to perform the impossible—to enter into every village, city, region, and continent and eventually unto the uttermost parts of the earth with the gospel of Jesus Christ. What a task for twelve men! Jesus pointed out their message and ministry and then backed it up with miraculous credentials only He could give. Their message was the gospel, the good news of salvation through faith in Jesus Christ. Their ministry was to share this gospel, their faith, with the whole world.

The commission given to the disciples was to carry on the identical work Jesus had done during His earthly ministry.

Jesus told the disciples in John 14:12, "Verily, verily, I say unto you, He that believeth on me, the works that I do shall he do also; and greater works than these shall he do; because I go unto my Father." Jesus was not saying that His disciples would do more amazing miracles. Can anything be more amazing than raising a man from the dead? Rather, the disciples, working in the power of the Holy Spirit, would carry the gospel of God's kingdom out of Palestine into the whole world. Isaiah 61:1-3 clearly defines every believer's commission:

> "The Spirit of the Lord GOD is upon me; because the LORD hath anointed me to preach good tidings unto the meek; he hath sent me to bind up the brokenhearted, to proclaim liberty to the captives, and the opening of the prison to them that are bound; To proclaim the acceptable year of the LORD, and the day of vengeance of our God; to comfort all that mourn; To appoint unto them that mourn in Zion, to give unto them beauty for ashes, the oil of joy for mourning, the garment of praise for the spirit of heaviness; that they might be called trees of righteousness, the planting of the LORD, that he might be glorified."

When the anointing of the Holy Spirit comes upon our lives as believers, we will reach the lost. We will reach those who are burdened and broken hearted. The Bible says that the Lord heals the broken hearted and binds up their wounds (Psalm 147:3). It is our responsibility to speak the message of Christ in our homes, our communities, our churches, and our world. We need far more than could ever be achieved with only user-friendly marketing skills. When we know the anointing and the filling of the Holy Spirit of God in our lives, the lost and needy will be irresistibly drawn to us.

The good news of the gospel is to be taken to those who are bound. Our world is filled with captives who are bound with sin and self and Satan. You and I have a liberating answer, the Word of God. John 8:32 says, "You shall know the truth and the truth shall make you free." Through the power of the Holy Spirit, we must take the truth to those who are bound.

We are also to take the gospel to those who are blind. In Mark 10, the blind beggar Bartimaeus cried out to Jesus for mercy. Many told him to be quiet, but that just caused him to cry out more. When Jesus called for Bartimaeus, Mark 10:50 tells us that ". . . he, casting away his garment, rose, and came to Jesus." There are multitudes of people who are blind and need to cast off their garments of sin and discouragement and defeat and come to Jesus. Jesus said, "He that cometh to me I will in no wise cast out" (John 6:37). To all those who are tired and weary, the Master still issues the call, "Come unto me, all ye that labour and are heavy laden, and I will give you rest" (Matthew 11:28).

Today we desperately need a fresh anointing of the Holy Spirit to penetrate the hearts of saints and sinners alike. It is our right and privilege as believers to exercise our God-given authority to be flaming prophets to a generation who needs to hear God's voice. We need the breath of God upon our lives so that we can confront the people as Elijah did on Mt. Carmel and say, ". . . choose you this day whom ye will serve . . . but as for me and my house, we will serve the LORD" (Joshua 24:15). Through the power of the Holy Spirit, the evidence of the reality of Jesus Christ will be seen in your life and mine. We must ask ourselves the question, "Have we lost sight of our calling and commission today? Is the Great Commission of preaching and teaching, binding up the brokenhearted, proclaiming liberty, and opening prison doors for those who are bound being carried out as it was given?"

As I go into different churches each week, I see people who are under great bondage. They are in God's house, but they are wounded and broken. Legalism has been preached instead of freedom, and they have been weighed down with guilt. Injury has been inflicted where wounds should have been bound. There is no oil of joy or garment of praise because there is the absence of the preaching of the good tidings.

Many of our colleges and seminaries today are commissioning young men into the ministry solely on the basis of theological supposition or doctrinal hypothesis. Some biblical scholars are more knowledgeable about exegesis than they are about Jesus. They can recite from memory the Apostle's Creed but are ignorant on the subject of winning the lost. They can convincingly argue the five points of Calvinism or oppose Arminianism but do not know how to deliver the captive from their bondage of sin. They have extended vocabularies and use phraseologies such as, " the anthropomorphic representation of the immutability of God," but it is beneath their dignity to say "Hallelujah" or "Amen. Praise the Lord." Perhaps they have never read Psalm 106:48,

". . . let all the people say, Amen. Praise ye the LORD." What does it avail if we are scholars in the fields of Pneumatology, Eschatology, Soteriology, Hamartiology and Ecclesiology, but lack the ability to comfort those who mourn?

The Bible says that God does not look on the outward appearance of a person, but He looks at the heart (I Samuel 16:7). It is possible to have every institutionally-required credential but lack the necessary spiritual essentials—the anointing of the living God. A parchment without passion is useless. Titus 2:14 says we are to be a peculiar people, zealous of good works. The call of candidates to the ministry should not be determined by the acquisition of a master's degree or even a doctor's degree, but by the degree to which they have met the Master. In my seminary classes I teach young men that they go to the Word of God, not to get a message, but to meet the Master. And when they meet the Master, they become the message. They become set on fire for the glory and honor of God and can say with Jeremiah, "His word is in my heart as a burning fire" (20:9).

In my travels it is not unusual to meet men like one discouraged young minister who related to me the events which led to his entering the ministry. He had graduated with a master's degree from a well-known theological seminary, having completed six years of study. He had been confident that he was adequately prepared for his first church. All too soon he found that he had all the right answers, but no one was asking the right questions. He quickly discovered that his parishioners were not even remotely impressed with all his intellectual knowledge. His eloquently prepared dissertation had centered on the dispensational divisions of human history, but no one requested his rhetorical hermenuetics. The little country church he was pasturing was made up of people who simply wanted someone to love them, feed them, comfort them, heal their spiritual wounds, and tell them about Jesus.

Jesus said in John 12:32, "And I, if I be lifted up from the earth, will draw all men unto me." More is taught by our lives than by our lips. Paul said in II Corinthians 3:2, "Ye are our epistle written in our hearts, known and read of all men." A modern translation of that could easily be these phrases I repeat to myself often, "You are writing a gospel, a chapter each day, by the deeds that you do and the words that you say. Men read what you write, distorted or true. What is the gospel according to you?" Precept must become practice. Illustration must lead to experience and indoctrination to inspiration.

Please do not misunderstand me—I am not against education. Much to the contrary, I favor it. I am the Dean of Liberty Baptist Theological Seminary. I hold a Bachelor of Science degree, two master's degrees, and a doctorate. My main objective in teaching is to introduce knowledge that leads to transformation of the heart. I have a little saying: *logos*, the Word of God, produces *ethos*, enthusiasm, which produces *pathos*, passion.

Referring back to the text that was quoted in Mark 6, let me now describe what I believe to be the most necessary ingredient for carrying out the Great Commission. Having considered the context and the commission, let us now consider the command in Mark 6:8-9, "And commanded them that they should take nothing for their journey, save a staff only; no scrip, no bread, no money in their purse: But be shod with sandals; and not put on two coats." What a seemingly preposterous command! Could this be right? Such meager provisions for such a great undertaking? Logic implies that the greater the task, the greater the need for provision. Inevitably the question arises how they could possibly survive on a long journey without adequate supplies.

Certainly Christ was mindful of his disciples' every

spiritual, physical, and emotional need. He would never forsake them. He knew exactly what they would need on such a journey. Imagine how you would feel if you were commanded to go on a journey, to travel by faith alone without benefit of any previous arrangements, accommodations, supplies, or even money. Extraordinary as it may seem, Christ chose only one item for their trip, "except a rod only." Let us examine this great commodity.

There was only one possession that Jesus deemed necessary for the journey to which he sent His disciples. That commodity was a rod. One might fictitiously wonder if the disciples silently questioned the Lord, "This old walking stick? Will this keep me warm on cold nights? Will it provide something to eat when I am hungry? Will it provide rest for my head when I am weary and worn?"

The Lord was not negligent concerning the needs of His disciples. They would soon learn that the rod they were told to take along on their journey was a pliable symbol of the Holy Spirit Who would prove sufficient for all their needs. The physical rod was the instrument Jesus used to teach the disciples the importance of leaning upon the spiritual staff, the spiritual power of the Holy Spirit. The purpose for Christ's unusual command was simple since the rod was such a prominent and practical implement in the lives of the disciples. It portrayed the spiritual power that was to come. Jesus was simply setting forth the fundamental truth for the ministry of the church.

Representative of the Holy Spirit, the rod was, and is, absolutely imperative for all Christian workers. God used the physical rod and staff, so familiar to the disciples, as a foreshadowing of the power that was to come. Jesus was not only teaching the early disciples dependence upon the Holy Spirit for power, provision, and protection, but He was also setting a pattern for servants throughout all ages. With this in mind, it is understandable how Jesus could make the promise to be with his followers always, even to the end of the age.

Today our needs are supplied through the power of the Holy Spirit of the living God. Paul put it this way in Philippians 4:19, "But my God shall supply all your need according to His riches in glory by Christ Jesus." What God's people held in their hands would soon be placed in their hearts through the indwelling Spirit to abide throughout the ages. Sending forth His apostles, Jesus had the power to provide for them with every material provision conceivable. He chose, however, to teach an unforgettable principle of truth—without the Rod of the Spirit all other means prove insufficient.

I am reminded of what Jesus said in John 15:5, "I am the vine, ye are the branches: He that abideth in me, and I in him, the same bringeth forth much fruit: for without me ye can do nothing." Without the power of the Holy Spirit, we can do nothing of lasting value. With the Rod, God proves to be our all-sufficient need. Through the power of the Holy Spirit, our sufficiency is of God (II Corinthians 3:5). The physical rod in the hand of each disciple was a picture of the believer in the forthcoming ages walking forth in service with the power and anointing of the Holy Spirit. We are admonished in Ephesians 6:10, "Finally, my brethren, be strong in the Lord and in the power of his might." What we need for effective ministry today is the endowment of God's power, the anointing of the Rod of the Spirit.

The missing dimension in many ministries today is their lack of power. Luke 24:49 states, "And, behold, I send the promise of my Father upon you: but tarry ye in the city of Jerusalem, until ye be endued with power from on high." The disciples were instructed to go to Jerusalem and wait for the arrival of the Spirit. In the present day church age, we need not delay or tarry for the promise of the Father for it has already come. At Pentecost the Spirit of God descended to take up His residence in the hearts of believers. He became their source of power, provision, protection, and presence. The only possible way we can effectively fulfill the command of the Great Commission is by the power given to us through the Holy Spirit.

Once the disciples recognized the Holy Spirit as Sustainer and Provider, Jesus permitted an enhancement of their ministries through the use of material provisions. This precept is found in Luke 22:35-36, "And he said unto them, 'When I sent you without purse, and scrip, and shoes, lacked ye any thing?' And they said, 'Nothing.' Then said he unto them, 'But now, he that hath a purse, let him take it, and likewise his scrip: and he that hath no sword, let him sell his garment, and buy one.'" Once the disciples had learned the intended lesson of dependence upon the Rod of the Spirit, they were then given the privilege of useful supplements. We need educated men in the pulpit, necessary tools to aid in the operation of the ministry, and funds to meet expenses. However, without the oil of the Holy Spirit, the machinery within the church produces little or nothing of eternal value. We must have God's holy unction.

Jesus emphasized the importance of venturing forth only under the authority and dynamic power of the Holy Spirit. "If we live in the Spirit, let us also walk in the Spirit" (Galatians 5:25). Not only do we suffer personally, but the church is ineffective when we lose sight of what God considers most imperative for ministry. When our priorities are out of order, we major on minor issues. So what tools does God declare essential for the task we are sent forth to accomplish? From this unusual message in Mark's gospel, we have considered the context, the commission, the command, the commodity, and now let us examine the consequence.

What were the results of the disciples' ministries when they traveled with so little? Were they successful? Did they lack anything? Were they in danger? What did they accomplish? As we have seen in Luke 22:36, when Jesus asked, "Did you lack anything?" They replied, "Nothing." The disciples' preaching led to men's repenting, the powers of demonic bondage being broken, and the sick being healed. Parallel to other Scriptural accounts, it is recorded that great miracles occurred as blind eyes were opened; the lame were made to walk; the deaf were made to hear again, and sinners were converted. Without doubt, the first evangelistic missionary preaching tour was an overwhelming success!

One example of the many successes within their mission can be found in Acts 3:1-11, where the first apostolic miracle occurred. Peter and John had gone up together to the temple to pray. A man who had been lame from birth was lying at the gate of the temple seeking alms. When asked for money, Peter replied, "'Silver and gold have I none; but such as I have give I thee: In the name of Jesus Christ of Nazareth rise up and walk.' And he took him by the right hand, and lifted him up: and immediately his feet and anklebones received strength. And he leaping up stood, and walked, and entered with them into the temple, walking, and leaping, and praising God. And all the people saw him walking and praising God" (6-9). Peter's powerful statement could be summarized by saying, "We have no money but we have the power of God." Today we find many churches with a full treasury but bankrupt of power. When the sick, lame, blind, and bound cry today for healing and deliverance, we offer them money. What a poor substitute! Praise God that a seemingly insignificant rod or staff continues to work today. It is working results in unbelievable success and faithfulness all over the world.

God uses people. Jesus invested His life in the lives of twelve men who turned the world upside down for the kingdom of God (Acts 17:6). How can we do less? These are critical days in which God uses faithful servants to perform His tasks. These servants may develop useful systems, but systems must never dominate God's servants. God always calls people and equips them with power to perform His calling. Dwight L. Moody once said, "God is always looking for men who are little enough to be big for God." If we as Christians will submit ourselves to the authority of the Holy Spirit through obedience to the Word of God, we will produce immeasurable results. My earnest desire is to see Christian's return to depending upon the power of God through the Holy Spirit so that they will know the joy and victory that only God can give.

Paul chided the Galatians when he said in chapter 3, verses 1-5:

> "O foolish Galatians, who hath bewitched you, that ye should not obey the truth, before whose eyes Jesus Christ hath been evidently set forth, crucified among you? This only would I learn of you, Received ye the Spirit by the works of the law, or by the hearing of faith? Are ye so foolish? Having begun in the Spirit, are ye now made perfect by the flesh? Have ye suffered so many things in vain? If it be yet in vain.

He therefore that ministereth to you the
Spirit, and worketh miracles among you,
doeth he it by the works of the law, or by the
hearing of faith?"

Paul confronted a serious problem in the lives of the
Galatian believers. They had been saved by the power of
God's Spirit but were attempting to be sanctified by their
own efforts. Paul confronted the folly of their thinking by
reminding them that what God had begun by the Spirit
could not be sustained by human effort.

Paul's indictment to the Galatians was direct because
the issue was serious. I believe it to be a timeless indictment
that relates directly to the church and to us as Christians.
Obviously, our culture and specific circumstances are different, but the problem of trying to perfect in the flesh
what was begun in the Spirit remains the same. We cannot
do in our own strength what only God the Holy Spirit can
do through us. It may surprise some to know that a believer may work very diligently, even sacrificially, but his work
be utter failure if it is done through human energy. All our
striving in self-effort is meaningless religious activity. I
cannot live a godly life for one hour without the control of
the Holy Spirit. Death to self and self-effort is my constant
heart cry.

I heard Joseph Carroll relate an experience of his that
illustrates a relevant point. While conducting a series of
meetings in both North and South Carolina, Joseph stayed
in the home of close friends in Asheville. He traveled each
night to his various speaking engagements. One night he
was scheduled to speak in a church in Greenville, South
Carolina, and since he did not have a car, some people from
Greenville volunteered to transport him to and from his

meeting. When they arrived to pick him up, he said farewell to his hosts and told them that he hoped to be back by midnight or soon afterward.

After ministering at the Greenville church, Joseph stayed a while to enjoy the fellowship; then he was driven back to Asheville. As he approached his hosts' home, he saw the porch light on and assumed that they were prepared for his arrival. He got out of the car at the end of the long driveway and sent his driver on his way saying, "You must hurry. You have a long drive back, and I'm sure they are prepared for me. I'll have no problem." He felt the bitter cold of the winter night as he walked the long distance to the house. By the time he reached the porch, his nose and ears were numb. He tapped gently on the door, but no one answered. He tapped a little harder and then even harder, but still there was no reply. Finally, quite concerned about the cold, he knocked on the kitchen door and then on the side window. No one responded.

Somewhat frustrated and growing colder by the moment, he decided to walk to a neighboring house so that he could call and awaken his hosts. Then he realized that knocking on someone's door after midnight was not a safe thing to do. So he decided to find a public telephone. It was very dark and cold, and he was not familiar with the area. Consequently, he walked for several miles. At one point he slipped as he walked in wet grass growing over the bank along the road and slid down into two feet of water. Soaked and nearly frozen, he crawled back up to the road and walked further until he finally saw a blinking motel light. He awakened the motel manager who was gracious enough to let him use the phone. Upon calling and waking his sleepy host he said, "I hate to disturb you, but I couldn't get anyone to wake up in the house. I'm several miles down the road at the motel. Could you come and get me?" To which his host replied, "Joseph you have a key in your overcoat pocket. I gave it to you before you left." An astonished and sheepish Joseph reached into his pocket and felt the cold steel of a key!

That story is a picture of many Christians. They want access into the house of blessings; they want comfort, warmth, rest, peace, nourishment, and fellowship. Yet they try to get in by human schemes, which ultimately fail. With all of their striving and self-effort, they overlook the key, the blessed Holy Spirit. He alone can relieve the frustrations and fulfill the deepest longings of man's hearts. "For he satisfieth the longing soul, and filleth the hungry soul with goodness" (Psalm 107:9). God provides everything we need for life and godliness. We need only to turn to Him.

Psalm 23 illustrates the sufficiency of God's provision to believers.

Verse 1

"The LORD is my shepherd; I shall not want." I can go to God for anything I lack, and He will supply my needs.

Verse 2

If I need food or water, "He maketh me to lie down in green pastures: he leadeth me beside the still waters."

Verse 3

If I am weak and weary, He restores my soul. He charts the course of my life and guides me in the path of righteousness for His name's sake. "He restoreth my soul: he leadeth me in the paths of righteousness for his name's sake."

Verse 4

Someday I will have to face the reality of death, but "Yea, though I walk through   the valley of the shadow of death, I will fear no evil: for thou art with me."

I am often distressed and in upheaval, but "Thy rod and thy staff they comfort me."

Verse 5

I am concerned about those around me who are hostile, but "Thou preparest a table before me in the presence of mine enemies." I need healing, and "Thou anointest my head with oil; my cup runneth over." It is a long life; therefore I want to make the best of it.

Verse 6

"Surely goodness and mercy shall follow me all the days of my life: and I will dwell in the house of the LORD forever." I desperately want hope after death. He promises that I will dwell in the house of the Lord forever.

Recently, this gentle reminder via email, with no credit given, touched my heart:

The Lord is my Shepherd—That's Relationship!
I shall not want—That's Supply!
He maketh me to lie own in green pastures—That's Rest!

He leadeth me beside the still waters—That's Refreshment!

He restoreth my soul—That's Healing!
He leadeth me in the paths of righteousness—That's Guidance!
For His name's sake—That's Purpose!
Yea, though I walk through the valley of the shadow of death—

That's Testing!

I will fear no evil—That's Protection!

For Thou art with me—That's Faithfulness!

Thy rod and Thy staff they comfort me—That's Discipline!

Thou preparest a table before me in the presence of mine enemies—That's Hope!

Thou annointest my head with oil—That's Consecration!

My cup runneth over—That's Abundance!

Surely goodness and mercy shall follow me all the days of my life—That's Blessing!

And I will dwell in the house of the Lord—That's Security!

Forever—That's Eternity!

Our shepherd graciously supplies everything we need. Why would we want to go anywhere else? Paul said, "And ye are complete in him" (Colossians 2:10). "Blessed be the God and Father of our Lord Jesus Christ, who hath blessed us with all spiritual blessings in heavenly places in Christ" (Ephesians 1:3). We have the promise in Philippians, "But my God shall supply all your need according to his riches in glory by Christ Jesus" (4:19). Christ has granted to us everything pertaining to life and godliness (II Peter 1:3). What a promise! Can it be that we have forgotten these provisions? How else can we account for so many Christians attempting to satisfy spiritual needs by human means?

As Christians, we easily fall prey to our own inadequacies and inabilities that increase our frustration and discouragement as we realize we can't solve our problems apart from God's Spirit. This is the truth God wants us to internalize. Until we come to an end of ourselves, we are of little use to God. He will spare no effort to bring us to the point of total surrender in our lives. When we reach this point and seek God with intensity, with our whole hearts,

we are then prime candidates for the blessed infilling of the
Holy Spirit of God.

The greatest men of God throughout the history of the
church have been men who sought God intensely, dedicat-
ing themselves to prayer and to the study of the Word of
God. They would accept nothing less than a life of intimate
communion with God. They knew that the Christian life,
which begins in the Spirit, can only be sustained by the
Spirit. One of the greatest theologians in the history of
Christendom was Aurelious Augustinius, better known as
St. Augustine. In agony of spirit, he prayed in his confessions, "Hide not Thy face from me. O, that I might repose
of Thee. Oh, that Thou wouldest enter my heart and ine-
briate me. Let me know Thee, O Lord, who knowest me: let
me know Thee, as I am known. Power of my soul, enter into
it, and fit it for Thee, that Thou mayest have and hold it
without spot or wrinkle. O my God, let me, with thanksgiving, remember, and confess unto Thee Thy mercies on
me. Let my bones be bedewed with Thy love, and let them
say unto Thee, 'Who is like unto Thee, O Lord?'"[1]

J. Hudson Taylor, founder of the China Inland Mission
and recognized as the father of modern missions, was a
man small in physical stature. He was far from strong and
faced many physical limitations, but he is described as
being a man who was, ". . . full of the Holy Spirit and of
faith, of entire surrender to God and His call, of great self-
denial, heartfelt compassion, rare power in prayer, marvelous organizing faculty, energetic initiative, indefatigable
perseverance, and of astonishing influence with men, and
withal of childlike humility."[2]

As a young teenage boy, Hudson Taylor wrote in his
journal, "Well do I remember how in the gladness of my
heart I poured out my soul before God. Again and again

confessing my grateful love to Him who had done everything for me . . . I remember as I put myself, my life, my
friends, my all upon the altar, the deep solemnity that came
over my soul with the assurance that my offering was
accepted. The presence of God became unutterably real
and blessed, and I remember stretching myself on the
ground and lying there before Him with unspeakable awe
and unspeakable joy. For what service I was accepted I
knew not, but a deep consciousness that I was not my own
took possession of me which has never since been effaced."[3]

The Holy Spirit glorifies Christ by revealing His majesty
and glory in Scripture and by producing Christ-centered
lives in believers. G. Campbell Morgan has said, "A man
full of the Spirit is one who is living a normal Christian life.
Fullness of the Spirit is not the state of spiritual aristocra-
cy, to which only a few can attain." A life that is focused on
knowing, loving, obeying, and serving Christ brings honor
to Him by displaying His characteristics to the watching
world. That is a life that shines forth as a light on a hill that
cannot be hidden. Matthew 5:16 describes Christ's desire
for our lives, "Let your light so shine before men, that they
may see your good works, and glorify your Father which is
in heaven."

I believe we are living in the last days before the return of
Jesus Christ. The harvest is ripe, but the laborers are few.
God needs men and women who will be His instruments to
reach a needy world. You and I will be those instruments
only as we walk with the Rod of the Spirit who enables us to
be available and effective for His service. God offers us the
power of the Rod today. We can accept Him or reject Him,
but whatever our decision, we will live out its consequences.

Called to the ministry many years ago, I felt the strong
tugging of the Holy Spirit on my heart and was eager to

learn what God required of me for full-time service. That discovery came early in my ministry when I learned that I was nothing, and that He was everything. God can and will use a man or woman who stands before Him empty hand-ed and says, "Lord, fill me. Oh, God, I am available to You. I have little to offer, but what I have, I give to you." Andrew Murray has written,

> "God does not ask you to give the perfect surrender in your strength, or by the power of your will; God is willing to work it in you. Do we not read: 'It is God that worketh in us, both to will and to do of his good pleasure'? And that is what we should seek for—to go on our faces before God, until our hearts learn to believe that the everlasting God Himself will come in to turn out what is wrong, to conquer what is evil, and to work what is well-pleasing in His blessed sight. God Himself will work it in you."[4]

Jesus faced the cross and offered Himself a sacrifice "through the eternal Spirit." He had no will of His own. So we, too, can be filled with Holy Spirit as we give up our self-life and come to the Lord in weakness and feebleness. God the Holy Spirit will provide the enablement if we will hum-ble ourselves and seek God's face. Remember:

> "When you do yield yourself in absolute surrender, let it be in the faith that God does now accept of it. Let each believe—while I, a poor worm on earth and a trembling child of God, full of failure and sin and fear, bow here, and no one knows what passes through my heart, and while I in simplicity say, O

God, I accept Thy terms; I have pleaded for blessing on myself and others, I have accepted Thy terms of absolute surrender—while your heart says that in deep silence, remember there is a God present that takes note of it, and writes it down in His book, and there is a God present who at that very moment takes possession of you. You may not feel it, you may not realize it, but God takes possession if you will trust Him."[5]

If you are a believer, your call today is to walk in the power of the Holy Spirit. Be assured that whatever God expects of you, and for every problem or enemy that rises up against you, He has lovingly and properly prepared you to meet the challenge with your rod in your hand which means the Rod in your heart. What peace and rest to know that the presence, power, and protection of the Holy Spirit of God are yours.

CHAPTER 4

THE RESULTS OF WALKING
WITH THE ROD
OF THE SPIRIT

We have seen that the apostles began their ministry with only a rod or staff. All their needs were met as they walked with that Rod. God endeavors to bring every true servant of Christ to the same level of dependence upon Him and His blessed Holy Spirit. Paul said, "I am crucified with Christ: nevertheless I live; yet not I, but Christ liveth in me: and the life which I now live in the flesh I live by the faith of the Son of God, who loved me, and gave himself for me" (Galatians 2:20). The dependence that Christ desires for every Christian is one in which a believer allows the Holy Spirit to control his entire life, thus providing him access to God. Access to God implies intimacy with God. Such intimacy means that a believer personally approaches

God without fear of rejection.

God is the provider of all spiritual resources. A man's deepest spiritual needs cannot be satisfied by natural means. Only God can satisfy those needs through the Holy Spirit. Andrew Murray has written, "What good does it do that we go to church or attend conventions, that we study our Bibles and pray, unless our lives are filled with the Holy Spirit? That is what God wants; and nothing else will enable us to live a life of power and peace."[1]

Paul said that God sent Christ that we might receive the adoption of sons. "And because ye are sons, God hath sent forth the Spirit of his Son into your hearts, crying, Abba, Father. Wherefore thou art no more a servant, but a son; and if a son, then an heir of God through Christ" (Galatians 4:6-7). As believers, you and I have come to know God and to be known by God. We are sons of God and son ship involves access and intimacy. The phrase "Abba, Father" in Galatians 4:6 is a term of endearment. Jesus cried out to God the Father in the Garden of Gethsemane when he prayed in agony, "Abba, Father, all things are possible unto thee; take away this cup from me: nevertheless, not what I will, but what thou wilt" (March 14:36). "Abba" is an Aramaic word and can be translated Daddy or Papa. It signifies a privileged family love. You and I have the privilege of approaching God the Father as we do our earthly father. This is what the writer of Hebrews had in mind when he said, "Let us draw near with a true heart in full assurance of faith" (Hebrews 10:22).

Paul emphasized the same truth in Romans 8:14-16, "For as many as are led by the Spirit of God, they are the sons of God. For ye have not received the spirit of bondage again to fear; but ye have received the Spirit of adoption, whereby we cry, 'Abba, Father.' The Spirit Himself beareth witness with our spirit, that we are children of God." Here in Romans 8, Paul uses adoption to illustrate the believer's new relationship with God. Likewise, when you and I accept Jesus Christ as Lord and Savior, we gain all the privileges and responsibilities of a child in God's family. One of the outstanding privileges of being a Christian is being led by the Spirit.

In Roman culture the adoptive person lost all rights in his old family and gained all the rights of a legitimate child in his new family. Under Roman law an adoptive child was guaranteed all legal rights to his father's property. He was not a second-class son. He was equal to any other son biologically or adopted into his father's family, and he became a full heir to his new father's estate. As adopted children of God, you and I share all rights to God's resources. Because we have full identity as God's heir, we can claim what he has provided for us. We may not always feel like we belong to God, but the Holy Spirit, the Rod of the Spirit, is our witness. His inward presence reminds us whose we are and encourages us with His love. "The love of God is shed abroad in our hearts by the Holy Ghost which is given unto us" (Romans 5:5).

What a privilege to be a child of the Master's instead of a cringing and fearful slave of sin. The day we got saved we received His best gifts—God the Holy Spirit living within us, the forgiveness of sins, and eternal life. God encourages us to ask Him for whatever we need. We have direct access to God through prayer. He is always available and approachable. We go to God the Father, not because we are worthy, but because He fully accepted the blood of Christ on our behalf. In fact, God bids us come boldly before Him in the time of our greatest weakness: "For we have not an high priest which cannot be touched with the feeling of our infirmities; but was in all points tempted like as we are, yet without sin. Let us therefore come boldly unto the throne of grace, that we may obtain mercy, and find grace to help in time of need" (Hebrews 4:15-16).

Let us not be guilty of looking elsewhere to have our needs met. Often we seem willing to substitute almost anything for prayer. The problem is our unwillingness to pray with intensity and wrestle with God over the issues of life. Communion with God is certainly worth our effort. Let us always remember the tremendous promise of God in Psalm 16:11, "Thou wilt show me the path of life: in thy presence is fullness of joy; at thy right hand there are pleasures forevermore."

David said, "One thing have I desired of the LORD, that will I seek after; that I may dwell in the house of the LORD all the days of my life, to behold the beauty of the LORD, and to inquire in his temple." (Psalm 27:4). That is a focus prayer that reflects David's longing to be in God's presence. David was desperate—not for what God could do for him or give to him, but rather for God Himself. He longed for intimacy with God. "Thy face, LORD, will I seek" (8).

The Psalmist in Psalm 42 displayed this longing as he prayed, "As the hart panteth after the water brooks, so panteth my soul after thee, O God. My soul thirsteth for God, for the living God" (1,2). These are the words of a man who is obviously in deep despair. Note that his solution was to seek God. In Psalm 73:25-26, Asaph said, "Whom have I in heaven but thee? And there is none upon earth that I desire beside thee. My flesh and my heart faileth: but God is the strength of my heart, and my portion for ever." He understood that earthly resources could not satisfy spiritual needs.

As Christians, we must always be reminded that God

alone is our source of spiritual power. Nothing can replace the spiritual power that comes only from long periods of communing with our living, awesome God. He is our life-line and source of strength. God's strength is available through the Holy Spirit. As we walk with our Rod, we are endued with strength to live a life of power and peace. "The joy of the Lord is our strength" (Nehemiah 8:10).

I have found that most people who come to me for counseling simply need a sympathetic ear and an encour-aging word from Scripture. As Christians, we need to bear one another's burdens (Galatians 6:2), and I am happy to share in that ministry. Sometimes, however, I think we can short-circuit the Spirit's ministry by turning to men before we turn to God. If someone feels better after simply talking to me, imagine how he would feel after talking to God! The Lord beseeches us to, "Call unto me, and I will answer thee, and show thee great and mighty things, which thou knowest not" (Jeremiah 33:3). We must call, and that involves time invested in a relationship with God over a long period of time, not just in times of trouble.

Prayer must be a two-way conversation. We speak to God in prayer, and He speaks to us through His Word. Illumination is the ministry of the Holy Spirit whereby He opens our minds to God's Word and makes it come alive to us as God speaks through its pages. I always talk to God with an open heart and an open Bible. As we pray, read the Word, and meditate upon it, God gives us wisdom to deal with the circumstances of our lives. Jesus promises, "If any of you lack wisdom, let him ask of God, that giveth to all men liberally [which means generously], and upbraideth not; and it shall be given him" (James 1:5). God graciously and willingly gives us all the resources and wisdom we need to live a victorious Christian life.

God desires that as Christians we be mirrors that reflect the glory of the Lord to a lost world. We can only do this as the Holy Spirit of God works within us, controlling our thoughts and actions. II Corinthians 3:18 says, "But we all, with open face beholding as in a glass the glory of the Lord, are changed into the same image from glory to glory, even as by the Spirit of the Lord." The glory that the Spirit imparts to every believer is even more excellent and lasts longer than that which Moses experienced in the Old Testament. Beholding the nature of God with unveiled minds, we can be more like Him.

Let me digress here to draw attention away from our own needs to the needs of a lost and dying world. Your desire and burden to win the lost to Christ will be in direct proportion to the control of the Holy Spirit in your life. After the Holy Ghost had fallen upon them, the disciples counted it a privilege to be a witness for Jesus Christ. A witness is someone who, perhaps simply but sincerely, tells another person what he has seen and heard. Threatened by the religious leaders of their day, Peter and John could say, "For we cannot but speak the things which we have seen and heard" (Acts. 4:20). As Christians we are not judges or prosecuting attorneys sent to condemn the world. We are witnesses who point people to Jesus Christ and tell lost sinners how to be saved.

You and I could never hope to fulfill the Great Commission apart from the empowering of our Rod, the Holy Spirit. On the day of Pentecost the Holy Spirit came upon the church and empowered them to preach the Word. After Pentecost the Spirit continued to fill them and anoint them with great power (Acts 4:33).

Witnessing is not something that we do for the Lord. It is something that He does through us. There is a great difference between a sales talk and a Spirit-empowered witness. People do not come to Christ at the end of an argument. Simon Peter came to Jesus because Andrew went to him and gave him his testimony. As believers, we must go forth in the authority of Christ's name and in the power of His Spirit, heralding the gospel of His grace. Our Rod, the Holy Spirit, is our strength to walk upright. He is a comfort to our hearts, a defense against our enemies, our Source of power to perform miracles, and our Supplier of all the spiritual water and bread that we will ever need. Just as the physical rod was the means by which shepherds and men of God rescued and saved lost sheep in Old Testament times, so we as believers rescue and save the lost today as we allow the Holy Spirit of God to control us.

In Romans 8:9, we see that every Christian possesses the Holy Spirit in all of His fullness from the moment he believes. There is no such thing as a Christian who does not have the Holy Spirit. "But ye are not in the flesh, but in the Spirit, if so be that the Spirit of God dwell in you. Now if any man have not the Spirit of Christ, he is none of his." If you do not have the Holy Spirit it is not because you are carnal or that you just have not received Him yet; it is because you are not saved.

Every Christian possesses the Spirit in His fullness. You do not get Him in bits and pieces, and you do not have to ask for more of the Spirit. There are often questions about what the baptism of the Holy Spirit means. Paul mentions this to the church at Corinth in I Corinthians 12. The Corinthians were carnal Christians; they lived like they were not Christians at all. Yet Paul said to those sinful Corinthians, "For by one Spirit are we all baptized into one body, whether we be Jews or Gentiles, whether we be bond or free; and have been all made to drink into one Spirit" (I

Corinthians 12:13). All believers have taken in the Spirit and have been baptized into the body of Christ. No Christian is excluded.

Then we must ask the question, "Are we ever commanded to be baptized with the Spirit?" Although there are several references to the baptism of the Holy Spirit in the New Testament, not one of them is a command. We are never commanded to be baptized by the Spirit since, as we have already proven, that this occurs when we are placed in the body of Christ at salvation. In addition, we are never commanded to be indwelt by the Spirit or sealed by the Spirit. These too are gifts from God at salvation. We are sealed, baptized, and indwelt all at the moment of salvation.

Galatians 3:27 says, "For as many of you as have been baptized into Christ have put on Christ." The question we must ask then is, "Is the baptism of the Holy Spirit an emotional experience?" Not necessarily. You may not feel it or know that it happens. Neither is it a physical occurrence. The baptism of the Spirit of God is the act by which the Holy Spirit puts you into the body of Christ. This happens when you believe, and it is a theological reality, not an experience. It may not involve feelings, but it is a fact none the less.

Let us examine the indwelling of the Holy Spirit. Paul had just finished dealing with the Corinthians concerning their immorality and fornication, when he said, "What! know ye not that your body is the temple of the Holy Ghost which is in you, which ye have of God, and ye are not your own?' (I Corinthians 6:19) He does not say, "Why don't you get the Holy Spirit so that you can get your life cleaned up?" In essence he says, "You must stop your immoral actions that are defiling the home of the Holy Spirit." Even when a Christian lives in sin, the Holy Spirit is there. He is a permanent resident in the life of every believer. The Holy Spirit can be defiled, grieved, and quenched (Ephesians 4:30; I Thessalonians 5:19).

It is interesting to note that just as Jesus commanded the disciples to wait in Jerusalem until they were endued with power, so you and I are commanded to be filled with this same power in Ephesians 5:18. In the Greek language there is an indicative mood that is a statement of fact and an imperative mood that is a command. It is a command to be "being kept filled" with the Holy Spirit. This is not an option or a suggestion for the believer.

What does it mean to be filled with the Holy Spirit? It means a moment by moment continuous action. The tense of the verb, present passive imperative, means being kept continuously filled with the Spirit. It is not a once and for all filling. It is to be done moment by moment. The passive voice of the verb indicates that something or someone fills you. You do not fill yourself. The Holy Spirit does the filling, and it is to be continuous.

There are several different uses of the Greek word *pleroo*, "to fill." One use has to do with pressure. The word *pleroo* is used of the wind filling the sails to move a ship along. Paul has in mind the idea that we are to be blown along by the wind of the Spirit of God and carried along the path that we are to go. By the power and energy of the Holy Spirit, we are to be carried along moment to moment, thought to thought, word to word, deed to deed, day by day.

Another use of the Greek word *pleroo* refers to permeation. Salt permeates so well that if enough is used, it will act as a preservative. Salt also serves to add flavor to food. In the same way, our Rod, the Holy Spirit, preserves and flavors the Christian life. This is what I call the fizzy principle.

A fizzy is a small tablet used to make a soft drink. It is like a flavored Alka-Seltzer tablet. Dropped in a glass of water, this small pill permeates the water, transforming it into a drink the same flavor as the fizzy. There is a sense in which the Spirit of God wants to flavor your life so that it will taste like the Spirit of God. I believe this is what Paul was referring to in II Corinthians 2:14-15, "Now thanks be unto God, which always causeth us to triumph in Christ, and maketh manifest the savor of his knowledge by us in every place. For we are unto God a sweet savor of Christ, in them that are saved, and in them that perish." When we are filled with the Holy Spirit, we will be a fragrance of Christ to all those around us, both the saved and the unsaved.

A third use of *pleroo* involves a sense of total control. Whenever a gospel writer wanted to refer to someone who was dominated by emotion he would use the word *pleroo*. Examples would include those filled with sorrow (John 16:6), fear (Luke 5:26), or madness (Luke 6:11). We see a correlation to how we live the Christian life. When self totally disappears and we yield to the control of the Spirit of God, we are filled with the Holy Spirit.

Jesus' life is the supreme example of One who lived a life of absolute surrender. Matthew 4:1 tells us that Jesus was led by the Spirit into the wilderness to be tested. Luke records the same incident and tells us that Jesus was full of the Holy Spirit as He was led by the Spirit into the wilderness (Luke 4:1). The condition by which the Spirit led Jesus was that he was full of the Spirit. Mark 1:12 declares that the Spirit drove Jesus into the wilderness because He was under the Spirit's control. Jesus yielded his life completely to the Holy Spirit—this is what it means to walk with the Rod of the Spirit.

The Lord appoints men filled with the Spirit when He

needs a job accomplished. In Acts 6 there was a need for men to serve over a ministry to widows. The disciples' criteria for these men included, ". . . men of honest report, full of the Holy Ghost and wisdom . . . and they chose Stephen, a man full of faith and of the Holy Ghost" (3,5). In Acts 7, before Stephen was martyred for his faith, Scripture describes him as a man ". . . full of the Holy Ghost" (55). After his conversion experience, Saul could not begin his mighty work for God until he was filled with the Holy Ghost, (Acts 9:17). God wants every child of His filled with the Holy Spirit.

You may ask how a Christian can continuously stay filled with the Spirit. Do we pray for the filling of the Spirit? Not necessarily. Since the filling of the Spirit is a command, I believe that God has given us all the resources we need to fulfill that command. God will accomplish His part if we will accomplish our part. He never asks of us something that He Himself will not give us. Our part involves a total emptying of self and a confession of sin. The filling of the Spirit involves a surrender of all that you are and all that you have. Complete surrender produces obedience to God and fellowship with Him in His Word and prayer every day. You cannot be filled with the Spirit until there is a death of self, a slaying of your own self will. Only when you are empty can the Holy Spirit fill you. Remember Paul's words in Galatians 2:20.

The filling of the Spirit is letting the Word of Christ dwell in you richly. The results of being filled with the Spirit are found in Ephesians 5 and 6. A person who is filled with the Spirit will have a continual song in his heart, quoting psalms, hymns, and sacred songs. He will be a deeply grateful person no matter what the circumstances of his life. A wife will submit to her husband, and a husband will love his wife. A child will obey his parents, and a father will not provoke his child to wrath. Servants will be obedient to their masters and masters will treat their servants kindly. Being filled with the Holy Spirit produces singing, giving thanks, submission, and right human relationships.

An amazing comparison exists between Ephesians 5:18 – 6:9 and Colossians 3:16–22. The lists are identical. The filling of the Spirit produces the same results as allowing the Word of Christ to dwell in you richly. Therefore, if we want to be Spirit filled, we must saturate our lives with God's Word. The Holy Spirit is the Author of the Word of God. Letting the Word of God dominate your life is to be Spirit filled.

The filling of the Spirit involves living each and every moment of your life as if you were standing in the presence of Christ. We see this illustrated in the life of Peter. When Peter was in the presence of Christ he did the miraculous (Matthew 14:22-33). He walked on the water of the Sea of Galilee just to be with Jesus. Peter not only did the miraculous, but he said the miraculous (Matthew 16:16,17). When Jesus asked His disciples, "Whom say ye that I am?" Peter responded, "Thou art the Christ, the Son of the living God." Jesus looked at him and said, "Flesh and blood hath not revealed it unto thee, but my Father which is in heaven." Peter also had miraculous courage. In John 18:10 we see Peter in the Garden of Gethsemane when Jesus was arrested. He took out his sword and was going to take on the entire Roman army single-handedly.

When Peter was separated from Jesus, however, he was a failure. How well we are acquainted with his denial of Christ. What happened to this powerful man who could walk on water, speak with divine inspiration, and exhibit miraculous courage? When he was removed from Jesus' side and separated from Him, He was a failure. But thanks be to God! Jesus did not leave Peter comfortless. We see in Acts 2 that after God the Holy Spirit filled Peter on the Day of Pentecost, he preached a sermon which resulted in the salvation of 3,000 people! Peter was saying the miraculous again. We see in Acts 3 that he began to do the miraculous again. On the way into the temple he allowed God to use him to heal a crippled man who had been lame for 40 years. And we see in Acts 4 that he had miraculous courage again when answering angry Jewish leaders.

The goal of our lives is to walk continuously with the Rod of the Spirit, which literally means that we are walking with Jesus Himself. Becoming Christ-like is a progressive experience (Romans 8:29; Galatians 4:19; Philippians 3:21; I John 3:2). As we study the Scriptures, our knowledge and understanding deepens, and the Holy Spirit changes us. The Holy Spirit reveals to us who Christ really is, and, in turn, the Holy Spirit reveals to us who we really are. The more closely we follow Christ by being obedient to His Word, the more we will be like Him. As we faithfully walk with our Rod, He will transform us into the image of God.

In I John 2:20 and 27, John said, "But ye have an unc-tion (anointing) from the Holy One, and ye know all things. But the anointing which ye have received of him abideth in you, and ye need not that any man teach you: but as the same anointing teacheth you of all things, and is truth, and is no lie, and even as it hath taught you, ye shall abide in him." The Holy Spirit abides within every believer as his resident teacher. The Greek word translated "anointing," *charisma*, literally means ointment, or anointing oil, and ointment is placed onto and absorbed into one's skin. The Holy Spirit inspired Scripture. He will, therefore, reveal questionable teachings to us and keep us from error and heresies. People who are against Christ are against the truth which the Holy Spirit reveals to believers. When we are led by the Spirit we will stand against false teachers.

To illustrate the Holy Spirit's unique qualifications for revealing the Word, the Apostle Paul compared the Spirit's knowledge of God's mind as a man's knowledge of his own mind in I Corinthians 2:11, "For what man knoweth the things of a man, save the spirit of man which is in him? Even so the things of God knoweth no man, but the Spirit of God." God's Spirit knew God's thoughts and revealed them in Scripture. The Holy Spirit illuminates God's thoughts in the minds of believers. You might ask, "So if God's Spirit is sufficient, why do we need God's Word?" The sufficiency of God's Spirit in meeting our needs does not mean we can neglect God's Word. Quite the contrary. The Spirit works through the Word to accomplish God's purposes in our lives. The more we study God's Word, the more opportunity we give the Holy Spirit to illuminate God's thoughts to us.

My Bible is my most prized possession. No words could describe its inestimable value to my life. The Bible is God's precious gift and message of love to a lost world. It is God's final, total, and complete revelation, His inspired, infallible, and inerrant Word. It has perfect unity. Written over a period of 1,500 years, it contains 66 books written by 40 different authors. Because the Holy Spirit oversaw the writing, the Bible is without one point of disagreement or contradiction. It is a book that is historically accurate. Throughout the ages historians have tried to discredit certain claims of the Bible, only to have an archeologist unearth evidence that vindicates God's Word as historically perfect in every detail. The Bible's extensive knowledge reveals facts about God that no man could ever know. It reveals facts about man that no man would ever admit. Read its pages to discover facts about the past, the present, and the future. Prophecies and predictions of the Bible come true every day.

The Bible is a scientifically-accurate Book. Several of our America's greatest presidents would have profited had their physicians not bled them but heeded the admonition of Leviticus 17:11, "For the life of the flesh is in the blood." William Harvey discovered that blood keeps a human being alive. When Jesus shed His blood on the cross for our sins, He was giving up His life for us. Job is the oldest book in the Bible. Scientists and religions that once claimed the earth rests on the back of an elephant should have read Job 26:7, "He stretcheth out the north over the empty place, and hangeth the earth upon nothing." Isaiah 40:22 proves that the world is a sphere; it is not flat as scientists proposed for years. Isaiah rebuked those who refused to believe God's Word, "Have ye not known? have ye not heard? hath it not been told you from the beginning? have ye not understood from the foundations of the earth? It is he that sitteth upon the circle of the earth, and the inhabitants thereof are as grasshoppers; that stretcheth out the heavens as a curtain, and spreadeth them out as a tent to swell in" (21-22). People have scoffed at the Bible saying that the stars sang. Scientists have now discovered that stars produce an illumination that can be picked up as a sound wave. The Bible is a marvelous Book, accurate in its every detail. God gave His Word to man to obey that man might know God and live a fulfilled life. Since the Holy Spirit, our Rod, is the Author of the Bible, He will guide us into all truth if we will allow Him to control us.

We all long for the day that we will be with Jesus. Until then, I hold the precious Word of God in my hands and the blessed Holy Spirit in my heart. A simple acrostic for the word BIBLE encourages me. The letter "B" stands for "brighten." In a dark world, the Word brightens my life. "Thy word is a lamp unto my feet, and a light unto my path" (Psalm 119:105). The letter "I" stands for "instruct." The Bible is my instruction manual for life. Order my steps in thy word: and let not any iniquity have dominion over me" (133). The second letter "B" in the word BIBLE, stands for "build." The Bible builds my life. My commendation for you is stated by Luke when he wrote, "I commend you to God, and to the word of his grace, which is able to build you up, and to give you an inheritance among all them which are sanctified" (20:32). The letter "L" stands for "liberate." The Bible liberates my life from sin and Satan. "Thy word have I hid in mine heart, that I might not sin against thee" (Psalm 119:11). "And they overcame him by the blood of the Lamb, and by the word of their testimony" (Revelation 12: 11). The letter "E" stands for "everlasting." Because God's Word is everlasting, my salvation, my hope, and my destiny are everlastingly secure. "Heaven and earth shall pass away, but my words shall not pass away" (Matthew 24:35).

I believe Psalm 19:7-9 is the single greatest treatment of the sufficiency of Scripture in the Bible: "The law of the LORD is perfect, converting the soul: [transforming the whole person] the testimony of the LORD is sure, making wise the simple [imparting skills for every aspect of daily living]. The statutes of the LORD are right, rejoicing the heart: the commandment of the LORD is pure, enlightening the eyes [enabling the believer to see truth clearly]. The fear of the LORD is clean, enduring forever: the judgments of the LORD are true and righteous altogether."

In this passage David uses six synonyms to describe

Scripture: law, testimony, precepts, commandments, fear, and judgments. Law refers to God's standards. Testimony refers to His self-disclosure. Precepts refer to life principles. Commandment refers to non-negotiable demands. Fear refers to instruction on worship, and judgments refer to God's verdicts on man's behavior. Scripture is sufficient to supply all God wants us to know about Himself and His will for our lives. Scripture must be illuminated and revealed by the Holy Spirit if we are to understand it. God's Spirit working through God's Word provides a supernatural resource that exceeds anything imaginable or conceivable on the natural plain.

How do you view the words of Scripture? Could you say, "More to be desired are they than gold, yea, than much fine gold: sweeter also than honey and the honeycomb" (Psalm 19:10). David prayed in that same chapter, "Let the words of my mouth, and the meditation of my heart, be acceptable in thy sight, O LORD, my strength, and my redeemer" (14). Is that your prayer? It will be answered only when you and I follow the command of Joshua 1:8, "This book of the law shall not depart out of thy mouth; but thou shalt meditate therein day and night, that thou mayest observe to do according to all that is written therein: for then thou shalt make thy way prosperous, and then thou shalt have good success."

In review, we know that when we became Christians, God's Spirit convicted us of our sins, brought us to repentance, and regenerated us. He then indwelt, baptized, sealed, gifted and separated us from sin. In the ongoing process of sanctification, He gives us access to God Who supplies all the resources we need for physical and spiritual life. The Spirit also illuminates our understanding of God's Word so that we are transformed by His principles as

He applies them to our lives. This is the process of walking with our Rod, the Spirit of God. He is sufficient for every need. It is our responsibility to be filled with the Spirit and to walk by the Spirit each day.

It is necessary to be reminded of these spiritual truths often because we quickly forget the source of our spiritual power. Many Christians are easily drawn away from depending upon the Spirit's ministry, focusing instead on some fast answer, some quick fix or panacea for their problems. The truth remains that if we would live a godly life we must move into the presence of God through prayer and allow His Spirit to minister to us and transform us through His Word. This is sanctification, the Christian's growing-up process.

What a tremendous privilege you and I have as believers to have direct access to God through the Holy Spirit in prayer. Do you daily take advantage of your privileged position? We must never let complacency and apathy rob from us the spiritual power and refreshment that comes from time spent in His presence. There is no substitute for prayer. If you have not developed or adopted a formula for prayer, one that is very helpful is the ACTS formula: A-Adoration: praising God. C-Confession: confessing sins. T-Thanksgiving: thanking God. Supplication: praying for others. Regardless of the pattern you use, be faithful and disciplined in prayer. It honors God and is your lifeline to a victorious Christian life.

We have seen that when we are walking with our Rod, the illumination of the Holy Spirit opens up our minds to God's Word and makes it come alive to us. As we communicate with God in prayer, He communicates with us through His Word. That is where we find God's answers to our questions and the solutions to our problems. Other solutions are helpful, such as seminars and counseling, but only to the degree that they are consistent with God's Word. Our first source of instruction and the standard by which we measure all others must be God's Word.

It is exciting and enlightening to realize that the Rod of the Spirit is indispensable. The Apostle Paul learned that there was no substitute for the dynamics of the Spirit that cause the heart to burn and faith in God to grow. He knew from the experience of many journeys and prison stays that the essentials of life are really few. Our bodies need some food, shelter, and clothing. Physically, we can survive on very little. Paul said, "I have learned, in whatsoever state I am, therewith to be content. I know both how to be abased, and I know how to abound: everywhere and in all things I am instructed both to be full and to be hungry, both to abound and to suffer need" (Philippians 4:11-12). We cannot long survive spiritually, however, without the living, dynamic presence of God filling us moment by moment. Paul said in II Timothy 4:16-17, ". . . no man stood with me, but all men forsook me. . . Notwithstanding the Lord stood with me, and strengthened me; that by me the preaching night be fully known, and that all the Gentiles might hear . . ."

Is your faith in God exercised only when every other alternate has been exhausted? How many of us find it necessary when we plan for a long trip to first count out several hundred dollars in cash to take along in case of an emergency? We line up our stack of credit cards to pay for everything from gasoline to dinner. Then we make sure they are safely tucked away. Is our membership to the AAA auto club still in effect? We double check on that before we run our car to the nearest garage to have a mechanic go over everything to make sure it is mechanically sound and the oil is changed. Once the travel route maps we ordered have arrived, we map out our trip, make motel reservations, and check the weather bureau for road conditions. Finally we are ready to venture out.

God help us in our "don't leave home without it" society that we plan our spiritual life with even greater attention. It seems that the priorities of the average Christian are in need of drastic revision. Pertaining to the needs of life, Jesus instructed us, "But seek ye first the kingdom of God, and his righteousness; and all these things shall be added unto you" (Matthew 6:33). All our vital necessities will be provided as we walk with the Rod of the Spirit. Happy is the heart who has learned to look to God for His power, presence, provisions, and protection.

CHAPTER 5

GOD'S ROD FOR HIS PEOPLE

Please focus with me again upon the scene in Mark 6: 7-13 when Jesus called the twelve disciples and sent them out on a gospel-preaching mission. As I pictured the apostles walking away from Jesus to begin their journey with only a rod in their hands, my eyes opened to a Biblical truth I had never seen before. Fascinated and challenged, I began to read through the Scriptures, realizing that every great man of God walked with a rod or staff in his hand. Before the Holy Spirit was given in Acts 2, all men of God carried a physical rod, staff, or stave as an outward sign to all nations and people that the Holy Spirit was dwelling upon them. Even though they did not have much knowledge about the Person of the Holy Spirit, it was He who came upon them and gave them power to perform the great works assigned to them by God. The physical presence of a rod in hand was a spiritual sign of God's presence. It was a continual reminder that apart from God they were helpless.

At Jesus' ascension, He told the disciples to go to Jerusalem and tarry there until the Spirit was given to them for their long journey of service. After the Holy Spirit was sent to earth in Acts 2, there was no need for a physical rod to be a sign. The Holy Spirit of God, their new Rod, would not only abide with them as believers, but He would indwell them. Today the Spirit of God does not come upon men with power to perform a certain task as He did in the Old Testament. Rather, as we have previously discussed, at the time of conversion to Christ, the Holy Spirit takes up His residence within a believer's life. The heart of the Christian becomes the temple of God. The Holy Spirit, the Rod of the Spirit, is absolutely essential for power and service to the Master. He is the Christian's strength to walk upright.

Let us now draw our attention to some men who walked with the Rod of the Spirit, because whom God employs, He also equips. Jacob was a great man of God whom the Lord used mightily. We see the Rod of the Spirit at work in his life. Genesis 32:9-10 tells us, "And Jacob said, O God of my father Abraham, and God of my father Isaac, the LORD which saidst unto me, 'Return unto thy country, and to thy kindred, and I will deal well with thee:' I am not worthy of the least of all the mercies, and of all the truth, which thou hast shown unto thy servant; for with my staff I passed over this Jordan; and now I am become two bands."

Jacob was renamed "Israel" because he was to be the father of a great nation. He served his time in the school of the Holy Spirit in the land of Padan-aram where he worked for his future father-in-law for 30 years. This schooling was necessary because Jacob was once very selfish, holding to a popular misconception that is still prevalent to this day—if you are to get ahead in life you must fight your way to the top regardless of whom you hurt. This philosophy holds that if you want the good things in life, you must lie, cheat, and steal to obtain them. Jacob wanted the blessings of Isaac, his father; so he planned a way to steal his brother Esau's birthright. In the twenty-seventh chapter of the book of Genesis the story of his deceit is recorded in graphic detail. After Jacob succeeded with his scheme, he ran in fear of his life, meeting his just reward in Padan-aram. He found that deception, double-dealing, duplicity, and guile was no way to prosper with God.

After long years in God's school, Jacob was ready to graduate with honors, awarded in the form of a staff. God had finally broken Jacob by humbling him and reducing him to a mere slave. He had sown to the wind and the whirlwind was Laban, a cunning and deceitful taskmaster. It was in that land of Padan-aram that God stripped Jacob of every earthly possession and honor and restored the staff or rod in his hand. He then had to return to his own country and face his brother, Esau, whom he had wronged and cheated many years before.

A broken Jacob returned to Esau to make restitution. What once was an attitude of pride, arrogance, greed, and deceit, had now been transformed to one of godly humility. God reassured Jacob that, with staff in hand, He would make his seed as the sand of the sea, which cannot be numbered (Genesis 32:12). Of all people, Christians should know that lying, scheming, manipulating, deceiving, and fraudulent acts never afford high positions of prosperity with God. With the Rod of the Spirit, our lives will be abundantly blessed. God longs to bless the righteous. "The LORD hath been mindful of us: he will bless us" (Psalm 115:12). Isaiah 1:19-20 declares, "If ye be willing and obedient, ye shall eat the good of the land: But if ye refuse and rebel, ye shall be devoured with the sword: for the mouth of the LORD hath spoken it."

It is interesting to note that once Jacob realized the value of the Rod of the Spirit, he gripped it tightly and securely for the rest of his life. We read in Hebrews 11:21, "By faith Jacob, when he was dying, blessed both the sons of Joseph; and worshiped, leaning upon the top of his staff." Within the words God chose to use in the pages of Holy Scripture, why would God direct the writer of Hebrews to mention such a trivial thing? Is it really trivial? This passage took on new meaning for me when I realized the rod's special place in the lives of Old Testament saints. I believe the rod again pictures the precious Spirit of God.

Jacob, old and weary, tired and feeble, had walked many a mile with God's Spirit as his aid. When he could walk no further, he did not cast his walking stick aside. Instead, he passed from this life into eternity leaning and resting on the precious old rod or staff. This scripture in Hebrews refers back to Genesis 47:31 when Jacob in his old age is facing death in Egypt. He asked his son Joseph to promise to take his body back to his homeland in Canaan for burial. "And he said, Swear unto me. And he sware unto him. And Israel bowed himself upon the bed's head."

Why is Genesis 47:31 translated as Jacob leaning on the head of the *bed* whereas Hebrews 11:21 is translated as Jacob leaning on the head of the *rod* or *staff*? Do not miss this very significant point. As Gleason L. Archer states in *The Encyclopedia of Bible Difficulties*, the Hebrew word for staff is *matteh*, which is the same Hebrew word for bed. The word for "bed" and the word for "staff" or "rod" are spelled exactly the same in the Hebrew consonants. Only vowel points first invented by the 8th century A.D., or a little before, differentiate between the two. The Septuagint, the Greek translation of the Old Testament translated back in the Third Century B.C., reads, *mattah* meaning, "staff." It was medieval Jewish Masoretes of the Ninth Century A.D. who decided it was *mittah*, meaning "bed." Hebrews 11:21 follows the earlier vocalization and comes out with a far more likely rendering, on the head of the "staff" like the Septuagint and the Peshitta.[1]

The point I wish to make is that the word *mittah*, meaning "staff," is also the Hebrew word for "bed." As we view the Old Testament staff or rod as having striking parallels to the Holy Spirit, is not He also our bed? We are called to rest in Him, to cast our every care upon Him, and to allow Him to sustain our whole weight. The entire book of Hebrews speaks of believers finding their spiritual rest. We read in Hebrews 4:9-10, "There remaineth therefore a rest to the people of God. For he that is entered into his rest, he also hath ceased from his own works, as God did from his."

The Apostle Paul says, "Be careful for nothing; but in everything by prayer and supplication with thanksgiving let your requests be made known unto God. And the peace of God, which passeth all understanding, shall keep your hearts and minds through Christ Jesus" (Philippians 4:6-7). When you and I are resting in the comfort of the Holy Spirit, we do not have to worry about anything. Paul's advice is to turn our worries into prayers as we rest in the power and comfort of the Holy Spirit of God. Then God's peace will come upon us, which is very different from the world's peace. True peace does not come from the absence of conflict. Abiding peace comes from knowing that because God is in control, our citizenship in Christ's kingdom is sure. Our destiny is set, and our victory over sin is certain. We can rest in the Lord because our Rod, the

Comforter is with us. What a beautiful insight when we realize that the words "rod" or "staff" and "bed" are the very same word in the Hebrew language.

Please allow me to digress a bit and consider the book of Hebrews, a book written to first century Jewish Christians to confirm that Old Testament Judaism had come to an end through the work of Christ. The key word in the epistle is the word "better." The writer states a series of contrasts between the Old Testament system of Judaism and the better things in Christ. One of these contrasts is to show New Testament believers the better rest we now have in the Holy Spirit. Hebrews 3:7-11 states, "Wherefore as the Holy Ghost saith, Today if ye will hear his voice, Harden not your hearts, as in the provocation, in the day of temptation in the wilderness: When your fathers tempted me, proved me, and saw my works forty years. Wherefore I was grieved with that generation, and said, They do always err in their heart; and they have not known my ways. So I sware in my wrath, They shall not enter into my rest." God repeatedly warned these Jewish Christians that their fathers did not enter Canaan's land because of their unbelief. Unbelief had no rest. They wandered in the desert wilderness for 40 years in a state of constant turmoil and unrest. If we would find rest today, it will be when we cease from self-effort and rely completely on the Holy Spirit of God.

The Holy Spirit is our bed and our staff or rod. He is our resting place where we may rest our complete weight on him. Entering into Canaan has always been viewed as a type of the believers' entering into the abundant, Spirit-filled rest and life. Jesus said in John 10:10, "I am come that they might have life, and that they might have it more abundantly." The only entrance into Canaan land is by the way of the Spirit. Flesh alone can never carry us into that blessed land. We must be transported by the Rod of the Spirit. I say without apology—salvation is a work of God, not an effort of man. "For by grace are ye saved through faith; and that not of yourselves: it is the gift of God: Not of works, lest any man should boast. For we are his workmanship, created in Christ Jesus unto good works, which God hath before ordained that we should walk in them" (Ephesians 2:8-10).

What a beautiful truth to know that my relationship with God is resting, not wrestling. The Holy Spirit is our Comforter, and in Him we may rest our full weight and struggle no more. The believer's service is not one of self-effort or a labor in the flesh. It is rather a sweet rest in the Spirit's power, which will carry us from one victory to another. Zechariah 4:6 says, ". . . This is the word of the LORD . . . Not by might, nor by power, but by my spirit, saith the LORD of hosts." In the Holy Spirit we as believers do not have to perform, attain, or work to make it through life's journey. We simply lean on the rod. Let us always remember Proverbs 3:5-6, "Trust in the LORD with all thine heart; and lean not unto thine own understanding. In all thy ways acknowledge him, and he shall direct thy paths."

The second person I would like to consider is Moses. Exodus 4:2 says, "And the LORD said unto him, 'What is that in thine hand?' And he said, 'A rod.'" Let us rehearse the story of Moses in Egypt. He had riches but no rod. As the son of Pharaoh's daughter, his life was one of ease and prosperity. Physically, Moses was a striking specimen of humanity, standing head and shoulders above other men. In the Old Testament account of his birth, we read that he was beautiful (Exodus 2:2). He was also very intelligent; it is recorded in Acts 7:22 that "Moses was learned in all the wisdom of the Egyptians, and was mighty in words and in deeds." He was not only a true scholar in his day, but he was a powerful leader as a man of action and authority. Tradition holds that Moses was appointed general over the Egyptian army.

Early in his adult life, Moses was not a prime candidate for God's service. His hands were so filled with worldly riches that he had no room to hold a rod. God cannot use a man with full hands. He desires a man who will come to him with empty hands that he might fill them. God does not normally call a man who has all the world's wisdom, riches, intelligence, and power. He usually calls a man who has nothing to offer so that there is no room for the man to glory in himself (I Corinthians 1:26-31).

The Corinthians were puffed up with pride (I Corinthians 4:6, 18-19; 5:2). The gospel of God's grace leaves no room for personal boasting. God is not impressed with our position, our power, our looks, our achievements, our degrees, our natural heritage, or our financial success. We do meet believers with high social standing, but there are not many of them. The description Paul gave of the Corinthian converts was certainly not a flattering one (I Corinthians 6:9-11). Paul reminded them that they were not wise, mighty, or noble. God called them, not because of who they were, but in spite of who they were. The Corinthian church was composed primarily of people who were terrible sinners before their conversion. This is an encouragement to us because we too were in a similar position to the Corinthians.

The Apostle Paul had been very self-righteous before his Damascus Road experience. He had to give up his religion in order to go to heaven. The Corinthians were at the other end of the spectrum, and yet they were not too sinful for God to reach and save them. They were the worst of the worst. There is no sin beyond the reach of God's grace.

Paul reminded the Corinthians why God called them. He chooses the foolish, the weak, the base, the lowborn, and the despised to show the proud world their need of His grace. The lost world admires birth, social status, financial success, power, and recognition, but none of these things guarantees eternal life. The message and miracle of God's grace in Jesus Christ astounds the mind, putting to shame the high and mighty people of this world. The wise of this world cannot understand how God changes sinners into saints. The mighty of this world are helpless to duplicate this miracle. God's foolishness confounds the wise. God's weakness confounds the mighty.

When we look back in the doors of church history, we see they are filled with accounts of great sinners whose lives were transformed by the power of the gospel of Jesus Christ. In my own ministry, as in the ministry of most pastors and preachers, I have seen amazing things take place that unsaved intellectuals could never understand. I have seen drug addicts, delinquent teenagers, and prostitutes become successful students and useful citizens. I have seen marriages restored and homes reclaimed, transformed by the Master Potter. Even my own life testifies of the mercy, grace, and miraculous intervention of the Lord. When I graduated from high school people said that I would be the one most likely to fail. God, however, put a new song in my heart so that many could see it and trust in the Lord.

God reveals the foolishness and the weakness of this present world's system so that no flesh will glory in His presence. My salvation must be totally of grace; otherwise God would not get the glory. It is this truth that Paul wanted to communicate to the Corinthians because they were guilty of glorying in men (I Corinthians 3:21). If we glory in men, even godly men like Peter, Paul and Apollos whom the Corinthians were honoring, we will rob God of the glory that only He deserves. It is the sinful attitude of pride that caused division in the Corinthian church and that we see causing division in our churches today.

Paul reminded the Corinthians of all they had in Jesus Christ. Every believer in Christ has all that he needs. Why should we compete or compare ourselves with each other when all that is good about us has been given to us and is due to the grace of God. The Old Testament prophet Jeremiah declared the word of the LORD who said, "Let not the wise man glory in his wisdom, neither let the mighty man glory in his might, let not the rich man glory in his riches: But let him that glorieth glory in this, that he understandeth and knoweth me, that I am the LORD which exercise loving-kindness, judgment, and righteousness, in the earth: for in these things I delight, saith the LORD" (9:23-24).

Through the power of the Holy Spirit, we as Christians share an intimate relationship with Jesus Christ. We find all we need in Him. He is our wisdom (Colossians 2:3); our righteousness (II Corinthians 5:21); our sanctification (John 17:19), and our redemption (Romans 3:24). Righteousness has to do with our standing before God—we are justified. God declares us righteous in Jesus Christ. We are also

sanctified—set apart to belong to God and serve Him. Redemption emphasizes the fact that we are set free because Jesus Christ paid the price for us on the cross. "Who his own self bare our sins in his own body on the tree, that we, being dead to sins, should live unto righteousness: by whose stripes ye were healed" (I Peter 2:24).

When Christ returns at the time of the Rapture, we as

Christians will experience our complete redemption. The three tenses of salvation are explained in the words just given. We have been saved from the penalty of sin—righteousness. We are being saved from the power of sin—sanctification. And we shall be saved from the presence of sin—redemption. This will be our glorification. Every believer has all of these blessings in Jesus Christ through the presence of the Holy Spirit Who is our Rod. We should glory in the Lord and not in ourselves or our spiritual leaders. We must allow the Holy Spirit, our Rod, to glorify Jesus Christ in everything we do.

Moses spent the first forty years of his life thinking he was someone very important, building up his life in worldly ways. In Exodus 2 we read of the impetuous action of Moses in killing an Egyptian. This led to his rejection by his own people the Israelites. It also eventually led to rejection by the Egyptians and the Pharaoh himself.

Moses' kingdom literally crumbled around him. He was forced to flee. Exodus 2:15 tell us, "Now when Pharaoh heard this thing, he sought to slay Moses. But Moses fled from the face of Pharaoh, and dwelt in the land of Midian."

God then took the next forty years of Moses' life to humble him so that He could use him. He started a process of demoting the man who would be king to the position of a servant. Moses was led to the wilderness where he became a common shepherd, learning to tread the desert sand until his skin was burned and his hair bleached with the desert sun. Moses exchanged the palace for desert sands, fountains of wine for mountain streams, and a scepter for a shepherd's rod. For forty years Moses lived a quiet and reclusive life far from the sumptuous splendor of eating at the king's table, riding in the king's chariot, and commanding the king's army. Moses no doubt suffered severe emotional distress as a marked man, his self image marred and his self-confidence lost.

What God perfected in Moses' life during those years was essential for the service He required of him. God sent Moses to school in the wilderness to strip him of every earthly possession, position, passion, and perspective before he could be God's chosen vessel to deliver Israel from Egypt. When he had lost it all, he was finally ready to graduate from the school of the Holy Spirit. In the hands of a bewildered, frail, defeated 80-year-old man, God placed his graduation diploma—a rod. From a burning bush on the side of the mountain, God called Moses to go back to Egypt to lead his people out of bondage. God was not through with Moses; he had prepared Him for great service. Exodus 3 records the intriguing account of how God rebuilt Moses' life. What took a lifetime to empty, God filled in a moment and asked, "What is that in thine hand?" And Moses replied, "A rod" (Exodus 4:2). I believe that at this point Moses was a little facetious, maybe thinking, "God, you call on me now? There was a time when I had everything going for me. I once had power and authority, riches and honor. I was able to speak eloquently. But Lord, after 40 years of tending sheep, living out here in the desert and talking to flee-bitten beasts, I have lost all my poise and dignity. Now you ask me what I have in my hand; well here it is. Just a shepherd's crook, this old rod, this worn-out stick. What's in my hand, Lord?" Moses was about to learn a lesson he would never forget. The rod was the sign of the power and presence of an awesome God. Psalm 110:2 says, "The LORD shall send the rod of thy strength out of Zion: rule thou in the midst of thine enemies." Moses never knew power until he laid Pharaoh's scepter aside and laid hold on the Rod of the Spirit.

In Exodus 4:3 God told Moses to cast down the rod or staff. When Moses obeyed, it became a serpent from which he ran. In verse 4, the Lord told Moses, "Put forth thine hand, and take it by the tail. And he put forth his hand, and caught it, and it became a rod in his hand." I believe there is something here that we should note. Moses had to determine what he wished to do with the rod in his hand. Held securely it would be the rod of power for the deliverance of the Israelites from the land of captivity, the means of Israel's salvation and deliverance from evil. When cast down, however, the rod was a vicious snake. The snake has always been a picture of Satan, the curse of sin, destruction, and evil.

In our lives today, we too have the opportunity to take the Rod of the Spirit in our hands and perform the great works of God. However, if we reject God's way and cast down the Rod, we open the door to evil and destruction. Jesus said, "He that rejecteth me, and receiveth not my words, hath one that judgeth him: the word that I have spoken, the same shall judge him in the last day" (John 12:48).

Moses fled from the serpent when he cast down the rod. Likewise, many who reject God's ways, spend their lives on the run. If you cast down God's precious, anointed rod, it will be to your own destruction. You will never experience victory. God warns, "Be sober, be vigilant, because your adversary the devil, as a roaring lion, walketh about, seeking whom he may devour: Whom resist steadfast in the faith, knowing that the same afflictions are accomplished in your brethren that are in the world" (I Peter 5:8-9). We must hold securely to our Rod to be victorious over Satan and his army. This is done as we are continuously controlled by the Spirit by being steadfastly obedient to the

Word of God. The sword of the Spirit, which is the Word of God, is our power.

Moses never cast the rod down again unless it was to show the power of God. He held firmly to the rod for the remainder of his days. In Exodus 4:20, after speaking to Jethro, his father-in-law, Moses . . . "took his wife and his sons, and set them upon an ass, and he returned to the land of Egypt: and Moses took the Rod of God in his hand." He returned to Egypt with the rod. God had instructed him in Exodus 4:17, "And thou shalt take this rod in thine hand, wherewith thou shalt do signs."

In Mark 16:20 Jesus said, "And they went forth, and preached everywhere, the Lord working with them, and confirming the word with signs following." This verse emphasizes Christ's power as well as His servanthood. Jesus' life and teachings turned the world upside down. The world sees power as a way to gain control of others, but Jesus, invested with all the authority and power in heaven and in earth, served others. As we walk with the Rod of the Spirit we will see miracles take place.

Let us review some of the miracles connected with the rod in the book of Exodus. It was the rod that Moses used to perform the miracles before Pharaoh that compelled Pharaoh to let Israel go. It was the rod that turned into a serpent before the eyes of Pharaoh (7: 9-10). It was the rod that turned the river of Egypt into blood (7:17,19,20). It was the rod that was stretched over the rivers and ponds of Egypt to bring a plague of frogs upon all the land (8:2-6). It was a rod that stretched out to smite the land of Egypt with plague of lice (8:16-17). It was a Rod of God that Moses stretched toward heaven and the hailstones fell on Egypt (9:23). It was the rod that brought the plague of locust (10:12-15). It was the rod that parted the water of the Red

Sea and gave the children of Israel access to cross over to Sinai on dry ground. The Lord said to Moses, "But lift thou up thy rod, and stretch out thine hand over the sea, and divide it: and the children of Israel shall go on dry ground through the midst of the sea" (14:16).

It was the rod that brought water from the rock in the wilderness. When the children of Israel lacked water and were ready to stone Moses, he cried out to the Lord and God said, "Go on before the people, and take with thee of the elders of Israel; and thy rod, wherewith thou smotest the river, take in thine hand, and go. Behold, I will stand before thee there upon the rock in Horeb; and thou shalt smite the rock, and there shall come water out of it, that the people my drink" (17:5-6). If we are to find the rivers of living water today, it will be through the Rod of the Spirit. In John 4:14 Jesus promised, "But whosoever drinketh of the water that I shall give him shall never thirst; but the water that I shall give him shall be in him a well of water springing up into everlasting life."

When Amalek came to fight with Israel in Rephidim, Moses told Joshua, "Choose us out men, and go out, fight with Amalek: tomorrow I will stand on the top of the hill with the rod of God in mine hand" (Exodus 17:9). It was the rod that was held by Moses on the mountaintop that caused Israel to prevail over the Amalekites. The rod represented the power of God over the enemy. If you and I are going to prevail over our enemy Satan we must stand and hold high our rod, the Word of the living God, the Sword of the Spirit. In his writings, the Apostle John said, "I have written unto you, fathers, because ye have known him that is from the beginning. I have written unto you, young men, because ye are strong, and the word of God abideth in you, and you have overcome the wicked one" (I John 2:14).

In the story in Numbers 21:5-9 we see an unusual use of the rod by Moses. Because of their constant murmuring against God and Moses, the Lord sent a frightful predicament against the children of Israel in the form of fiery serpents. Poisonous snakes bit the people, and many of them died. After the people acknowledged their sin and asked Moses to pray, God offered a solution. He told Moses to make a bronze serpent and put it on a pole. Even though they had been bitten, those who looked up at the fiery serpent would live. You have probably read and heard many spiritual applications concerning the bronze serpent. Some view it as a symbol of sin and judgment. Many times it has been equated with Christ who was made sin for us and placed upon the cross to die for our sins. The medical profession uses a snake on a pole as its symbol of healing. As we look to Him, He provides healing and forgiveness of our sins, as well as eternal life.

As I considered the word "pole" upon which Moses placed the bronze serpent, I found it to simply mean a hand-held stick or portable standard on which a flag might be carried into battle. Moses made a bronze serpent, fastened it to his rod, and held it before the people to look to for healing. The spiritual application is obvious. The stick held up or supported the bronze serpent. "And as Moses lifted up the serpent in the wilderness, even so must the Son of man be lifted up" (John 3:14). If Christ would be lifted up, it is through the Holy Spirit. Jesus said in John 15:26, "But when the Comforter is come, whom I will send unto you from the Father, even the Spirit of truth, which proceedeth from the Father, he shall testify of me." The Spirit of truth," that is our rod, testifies of Jesus Christ. In John 12:32 Jesus said, "And I, if I be lifted up from the earth, will draw all men unto me." The Holy Spirit has come to glorify and exalt Jesus Christ and His work on the cross. Moses could not lift up the bronze serpent without a rod or standard; so also Christ will not be lifted up or exalted by the arm of the flesh. There is not a preacher, evangelist, singer, choir, or church that can exalt Christ without the rod of the standard of the Holy Spirit.

The present day ministry of the Holy Spirit is to place Christ on display before men. Paul said, "Not that we are sufficient of ourselves to think any thing as of ourselves; but our sufficiency is of God" (II Corinthians 3:5). As Christians, we are not fit or qualified to claim anything as coming from ourselves for our power is in Christ through the Holy Spirit. The Rod of the Spirit will raise up Christ in full view of men that they might look to Jesus and live. Paul complimented the church at Corinth when he said, "Ye are our epistle written in our hearts, known and read of all men" (II Corinthians 3:2). As we walk with our Rod, Christ will be lifted up in us and through us, and we will display the fruit of the Spirit to a lost world. Christ will be lifted up by no other means than the Holy Spirit.

Let us go on to another example of the Rod of the Spirit in the Old Testament—the exodus of the children of Israel from Egypt. There is no record in the Old Testament that paints a more vivid picture or type of the redemptive work of Christ than we see in the book of Exodus. Exodus, which means exit or departure, is a fitting title for the book which describes the going out of the chosen people from the land where they were held in bondage and slavery for generations. The book is filled with precious types of Christ and his spiritual work of salvation in the heart of the believer. It presents rich symbolic meaning in the Passover, manna, Egypt, the rock, the Tabernacle, and Moses himself.

In the book of Exodus, we see God at work in the lives

of the children of Israel who were held in bondage in the land of Egypt. Pharaoh had resisted God for as long as he could. The plagues were increasing with such intensity that Pharaoh finally conceded to let Israel go. The plague that would break Pharaoh's stubborn will was the death of the first born in Egypt. God provided a way for the Israelites to be protected from this plague of death. It was the Passover. In Exodus 12 we have the account of the sacrifice of the Passover lamb. The blood was to be applied to the door-post of each house wherein a believing family dwelt. They were instructed to gather all their households under one roof and eat the flesh of the sacrificial lamb. They were to be ready for immediate travel, for they were to leave in haste at God's command. The Lord commanded in Exodus 12:11, "And thus shall ye eat it; with your loins girded, your shoes on your feet, and your staff in your hand; and ye shall eat it in haste: it is the LORD'S Passover."

Not only is Christ and His sacrifice as our Passover Lamb portrayed in the Old Testament book of Exodus, but there is also the mention of the rod. The Holy Spirit is once again typified as the walking stick. The Israelites were instructed to remember to take their rods in their hands for their journey out of Egypt. When you and I were called out of this world and released from the bondage of sin and death, we are also instructed to take the Rod in hand. Remember Ephesians 5:18 which says, "And be not drunk with wine, wherein is excess; but be filled with the Spirit." The Bible says we are to walk in the Spirit. "Walk in the Spirit, and ye shall not fulfill the lust of the flesh" (Galatians 5:16). "If we live in the Spirit, let us also walk in the Spirit" (Galatians 5:25). When you and I walk in the Spirit we will journey victoriously, possessing the necessary power to separate ourselves from the world. Without the power of our Rod, the Holy Spirit, we will be side tracked and defeated by Satan.

I see many Christians foolishly endeavoring to make the great escape from the world solely on foot, the foot of the flesh. This is absolutely preposterous. It is like trying to fly without a plane, cross the Atlantic without a ship, or climb the Swiss Alps without a rope. When will Christians realize that the deliverance from the things of this world demands the use of the Rod of the Spirit? We must walk in the Spirit daily. Paul said, "I die daily" (I Corinthians 15:31). Jesus told His disciples, "If any man will come after me, let him deny himself, and take up his cross, and follow me" (Matthew 16:24). Most Christians feel that if they have been saved and have applied the blood of the Passover lamb to their lives that they are automatically delivered from the bondage of sin and slavery. This is not true. Deliverance will not come until we secure the Rod.

The great Apostle Paul came to this realization in Romans 7 and 8. He speaks of the frustrating grip of sin: "I am carnal, sold under sin. For that which I do, I allow not: for what I would, that do I not; but what I hate, that do I. If then I do that which I would not, I consent unto the law that it is good. Now then it is no more I that do it, but sin that dwelleth in me. For I know that in me [that is, in my flesh,] dwelleth no good thing: for to will is present with me; but how to perform that which is good I find not. For the good that I would, I do not: but the evil, which I would not, that I do. Now if I do that I would not, it is no more I that do it, but sin that dwelleth in me" (Romans 7:14-20). In verse 24 he says, "O wretched man that I am! Who shall deliver me from the body of this death?" The answer is to get hold of the Rod of the Spirit and never let Him go. "I thank God through Jesus Christ our Lord" (25).

Most Christians realize the truth of Romans 6. Our problem is that the fleshly nature drags us down and tries to enslave us. The flesh generates evil. Not many Christians, however, understand or have entered into the experience of chapter 7. This involves the human realization that we as finite human beings are not good. Most Christians live in the law. They have a series of rules and regulations that they regularly obey in the energy of the flesh. They call this dedicated Christian living. The flesh enjoys being religious and trying to obey laws and rules. The most deceitful thing about the flesh is that it can appear spiritual, when in reality the flesh is at enmity with God.

Romans 7 deals with the law as it generates good. Two aspects of the cross lend insight here. The cross of Christ means much more than salvation from sin. Because of the cross, it is possible for me to reign in life and to have victory in peace and power. The phrase "the flesh" does not mean the physical body as such, but rather the very nature of man apart from God's influence and power. Other terms used for the flesh are the "old man," "the body of sin," and "the self." Everything the Bible says about the flesh is negative. Until the believer admits that he cannot control the flesh, change the flesh, cleanse the flesh, or conquer the flesh in himself, he will never enter into the life and liberty of Romans 8.

In Philippians 3 we see Paul, the perfect Jew, "Circumcised the eighth day, of the stock of Israel, of the tribe of Benjamin, an Hebrew of the Hebrews; as touching the law, a Pharisee" (5) saying, "Though I might also have confidence in the flesh. If any other man thinketh that he hath whereof he might trust in the flesh, I more" (4). Paul learned and indicates in Romans 7 that even his flesh was not subject to God's law. Perhaps he did not commit the outward acts of sin, but he certainly cherished the inward attitudes. The law of God is certainly holy and good, but a holy law can never control sinful flesh. This truth, that the Christian life cannot be lived in the energy of flesh that attempts to do good works for God, comes as a shock even to well-taught believers. No believer on earth can ever do anything in the flesh, however religious, that will please God. What a tragedy to live under the bondage of laws, rules, and regulations when we have been called into glorious liberty through the Spirit.

Let us look at the believer's responsibility in living a holy life. Christian living is not a passive thing in which we merely die and let God do everything. Three key words of chapter 6 are "know," "reckon," and "yield." We must know our spiritual position and privileges in Christ. This involves spending time in the Word of God. We must reckon, or count, that what God says about us in the Bible, is true. Finally, we must yield all to the Spirit. This does not involve just once a week or even just once at the beginning of each day. This is a moment-by-moment process all day long. This is what it means to walk in the Spirit (Galatians 5:25). The old nature strongly wants to do evil, and the flesh is weak when it comes to doing anything spiritual. We must feed the new nature on the milk, meat, bread and the honey of the Word of God. We must reckon the old nature to be dead. Why feed a dead man? Yet, many Christians feed the old nature on the husks of the world and the flesh, while the new nature starves for manna from God and fellowship with God in prayer. God has already done His part. Our responsibilities are clear: know, reckon and yield to the power and leadership of the Holy Spirit through the instrument of the Word of God.

The believer has two dispositions. One leads toward the things of the flesh, producing a carnal Christian who is at enmity with God. The other is inclined to the things of the Spirit, producing a spiritual Christian whose life is filled with joy and peace. The carnal Christian cannot please God. He is one who chooses to walk in his own ways instead of choosing to walk with the Rod of the Spirit in God's ways. The Christian has no obligation to the flesh. "Therefore, brethren, we are debtors, not to the flesh, to live after the flesh" (Romans 8:12). Our debt and obligation is to the Holy Spirit.

The Holy Spirit convicted us of sin and showed us our need of the Savior. He imparted saving faith and the new nature within us. Daily the Spirit witnesses and confirms with our spirit that we are God's children. What a great debt we owe the Spirit! Christ loved us so much He died for us. The Spirit loves us so much that He lives in us. He endures our carnality, selfishness, and pride. Daily He is grieved and quenched by our sin, yet He remains in us as a seal of God and a down payment of the blessings that await us in eternity.

The Holy Spirit leads us into a glorious life of liberty in Christ. II Corinthians 3:17 says, ". . . where the Spirit of the Lord is, there is liberty." Liberty to the believer does not mean freedom to be what we please, for that is the worst kind of slavery. Rather, Christian liberty in the Spirit is freedom from law and the flesh so that we can please God and become what He wants us to be. His ultimate goal for each of us is to be just like Jesus. Every believer is a child of God by birth and an heir of God through adoption. What an amazing thought to know that we are joint heirs with Christ, so much so that He cannot receive His inheritance in glory until we do. Thank God! As believers, we have no obligation to the flesh, to feed it, pamper it, or obey it. Instead we must put to death (mortify), the deeds of the flesh by the power of the Spirit (Romans 8:13, Colossians 3:9) and allow the Spirit to direct our lives daily as we walk with our Rod.

Let us emphasize again that it is our responsibility to walk with the Lord daily, all day long, as we yield to the leadership of the power of the Holy Spirit. The Israelites had a long journey from Egypt to Canaan, and the only way they could successfully move ahead was through the use of the rod. They stepped out by faith. Although every believer holds the Rod of the Spirit in his hand, many know nothing of its power. They wander through the wilderness of sin and defeat never appropriating the Rod of the Spirit Who enables them to cross the spiritual Jordan into the abundant Christian life.

The activities of the Israelites in the wilderness wanderings portray what many of us see happening in our churches today. A multitude of fleshly manifestations include doubt, fear, unbelief, murmuring, rebellion against spiritual leadership, and carnality. It was a relatively short journey from Egypt to Canaan, but it took Israel forty years to get there. They were under the blood, had salvation, and went through the waters of baptism, but they were not in the Spirit. Never forget Romans 8:8, "So then they that are in the flesh cannot please God."

If we as Christians would stop fussing about when you get "it," how you get "it," and who gets "it," we could saturate our lives with the Word of God and begin to walk in the Spirit and experience victory in our lives. Before I die, I would like to see the victory and power of Pentecost. This will only happen as we Christians become united in our love for Christ and one another. For too long we have disputed and fussed and fought with one another over theological terms. One camp is so avid in their emphasis of the Spirit that the Father and Son are neglected, producing an imbalance. The other camp is so opposed to the emphasis of the Spirit that they grieve the Spirit. Some swing from one extreme to the other and never seem to strike a balance.

Truth out of balance will always produce error. Jesus set the balance well when he said in John 4:24, "God is a Spirit: and they that worship him must worship him in spirit and in truth." Truth without spirit is dead and void. It will kill. Paul said in II Corinthians 3:6, "Who also hath made us able ministers of the new testament; not of the letter, but of the spirit: for the letter killeth, but the spirit giveth life." The spirit without truth is chaotic and erroneous and will quickly lead to division, strife, and vainglory.

Many Christians long to see some life and freshness in the church. They hear the Word of God preached and taught, dissected, expounded, and examined; but there is no true worship filled with life, joy, power, and praise. On the other hand, there are services where, in the name of freedom of worship, there are eruptive and emotional outbursts that are merely carnal demonstrations of the flesh. Believers in those services long for structure, organization, and leadership, but most importantly, for the truth of the Word of God. As I have served God for over two decades now, I see how desperately God's people are crying out for balance.

I pastored Open Door Baptist Church in Tuscaloosa, Alabama, for 14 years. I humbly and truthfully can say that our church gave a balance of Spirit and truth to the people of Tuscaloosa County. We saw a group of 35 people become an active membership of over 2,000, averaging over a thousand on Sunday mornings in Sunday school and

1,200 to 1,500 people in our worship service. We witnessed a beautiful balance of what it means to worship God in Spirit and in truth, through music and praise and in the teaching of the Word of God. Every year God blessed us with between 200 to 300 people who were saved and baptized. God longs to manifest His presence in a church filled with members who are walking with the Rod of the Spirit, the blessed Holy Spirit of Truth.

I was invited to preach, on several occasions, at Zion Baptist Church in Clarion, PA. Shortly after hearing the message on the Rod of the Spirit, Nancy Lewis, a member of the church, wrote a beautiful poem, which so adequately portrays the truths of this message.

The Rod and the Spirit

Let's compare in the Scriptures both the Old and the New
    what the Rod and the Spirit mean to you.
They seem like they're different; yet they're the same,
    used by God for his glory so that man He could gain.
Jacob lied, and he schemed and was a deceitful man,
    until God with a rod brought forth his new plan.
If your life is like Jacob's, you'll reap what you sow.
    But the Spirit longs to take control when you're brought low.
Moses lived in a palace, rode a chariot of the king.
    God emptied his hands so to the rod he would cling.
Are we searching for riches, for glory and fame?
    Holy Spirit take it all until we're never the same.
Many miracles were wrought with the rod we are told,
    As the children of Israel stood before the Pharaoh of old.
The Spirit's been moving, and God is answering prayer,
    Deliver us all from the enemy's snare.
With rod in hand, Gideon won a great war,

    Though his army was few and the enemy more.
We are never outnumbered with God on our side.
    Any battle can be won when the Spirit is our Guide.
Goliath stood tall, and at David he would laugh,
But David prevailed with his sling and his staff.
Though trials and temptations seem awesome and great,
With the Spirit within us we are free of all hate.
The spies came back with gripes on their tongues;
Yet their grapes were so big on the rod they were hung.
For us today there's a Canaan land, too.
Let the fruit of the spirit grow abundantly in you.
Joshua's rod went willingly out,
To be through with one be a trump and a shout.
The strongholds around us will crumble and fall;
Just yield to the Spirit and heed to His call.
Do you feel you are not worthy like these men of old?
It was a rod in their hand that made them so bold.
Let the Spirit take over and have His own way,
And you'll find new victory; it can happen today.

CHAPTER 6

THE SPIRIT'S ROD TURNS TRIALS TO TRIUMPHS

There is no doubt in my mind that each one of you reading this page will experience some kind of tragedy in your life before God takes you home. Some people seem to endure one tragedy after another their entire lives. Scripture instructs us, "Man is born unto trouble, as the sparks fly upward" (Job 5:7); "Man that is born of a woman is of few days and full of trouble" (Job 14:1); "And though the Lord give you the bread of adversity, and the water of affliction, yet shall not thy teachers be removed into a corner any more, but thine eyes shall see thy teachers" (Isaiah 30:20); "When thou passest through the waters, I will be with thee; and through the rivers, they shall not overflow thee: when thou walkest through the fire, thou shalt not be burned; neither shall the flame kindle upon thee" (Isaiah 43:2). We have certainly not been promised a life exempt from heartache and troubles.

After the Apostle Paul's conversion, the Lord told him that he would suffer many things for the Lord's sake. In the latter years of his life he knew his destiny involved suffering. In Acts 20: 22-23 Paul tells concerned fellow saints, "And now, behold, I go bound in the spirit unto Jerusalem, not knowing the things that shall befall me there: Save that the Holy Ghost witnesseth in every city, saying that bonds and afflictions abide me." Paul knew he was being irresistibly drawn toward Jerusalem. In verse 23 he says that the Holy Spirit told him that suffering awaited him.

Paul did not run from suffering. He accepted and actually welcomed it as an identification with Christ. Paul never ceased thanking God for saving him and making Him His heir. He spoke of being " . . . heirs of God, and joint-heirs with Christ; if so be that we suffer with him, that we may be also glorified together. For I reckon that the sufferings of this present time are not worthy to be compared with the glory which shall be revealed in us" (Romans 8:17-18). Paul prayed to know the fellowship of Christ's suffering (Philippians 3:10), and whether beaten, jailed, or left for dead, he rejoiced that he was counted worthy to suffer shame for the name of Jesus Christ.

Perhaps it is the pampered age in which we live. Maybe it is our comfortable lifestyles. The sad truth remains that most American Christians have no concept of the word "suffering," and faced with the slightest amount of it, we begin to murmur and question God. Where are the Hebrews 11 saints today, those who were destitute, afflicted, tormented, "Of whom the world was not worthy . . ." (38)? Martyrdom certainly is prevalent in our day and age, but it is mostly experienced in countries far from ours. Somehow that seems distant and unreal to us, who prefer to stay centered in our own little worlds. To most of us, the

Bible is a "me" Book—bless my life as I read your Word today, God; give me what I want, God; make me happy, God.

Some want to be free of trouble so that God can "use" them. Does God use saints whose lives are free of trouble? We know that God has chosen people to do His bidding on this earth, although He does not need the help of men. He could do the work Himself, but when he has a job that He wants done, He looks for a man or a woman whom He can trust. He looks for a human vessel through whom He can accomplish His purposes.

1 Corinthians 3:9 says, "For we are laborers together with God: ye are God's husbandry, ye are God's building." "We then, as workers together with him, beseech you also that ye receive not the grace of God in vain" (II Corinthians 6:1). The word of the Lord came to Ezekiel and said, "And I sought for a man among them, that should make up the hedge, and stand in the gap before me for the land, that I should not destroy it: but I found none" (22:30). God blesses and works through individual men and women. When godly men and women are blessed, so are the organizations, networks, churches, denominations, and even nations with which they are associated.

Does God look for great men and women through whom to accomplish His work? No, God does not look for mighty men, wise men, or noble men. He looks for the foolish, the weak, and the despised (I Corinthians 1:26-29). God longs for empty vessels that are available to Him. Men whose hands are full of mundane resources will not have room to hold the rod. So it is not a question of man's ability but of his poverty. It is not what we bring with us but what we allow God to put within us that matters.

Let us look at a story in Judges 6 to lend insight into

this matter. The children of Israel were in trouble once again. Because of their sin, God had allowed them to be devastated and plundered by the Midianites for seven years. After crying out to the Lord, God purposed to set them free from the oppression of their enemy. He sent an angel to speak to Gideon and call him to rescue His children. Gideon, however, had many doubts and asked many questions. He could not understand how he could save Israel. He was from one of the poorest families in the whole tribe of Manasseh and the least thought of in his entire family. Gideon asked for a sign to confirm that it truly was Jehovah God Who was speaking to him through an angel. After he had prepared a present, Judges 6:21 tells us, "Then the angel of the LORD put forth the end of the staff that was in his hand, and touched the flesh and the unleavened cakes; and there rose up fire out of the rock, and consumed the flesh and the unleavened cakes. Then the angel of the LORD departed out of his sight."

When Gideon saw just a rod, a plain stick, in the angel's hand, he must have thought, "A stick, a rod? What are you going to do with that? How could that help in beating off a million and one Midianites?" In response God might have said, "But Gideon, you don't know what's in that stick, that rod. It is the rod of the Spirit." It is as if God was saying to Gideon. "Here son, let me show you how it works." And work it did! Not only was the present consumed, but God brought a great victory to a man with a rod in his hand. Recall if you will how God told Gideon that the army of Israel was too large. Gideon started with 32,000 men, and God reduced the army to 300 soldiers with no conventional weapons. In Judges 7:2 the Lord said to Gideon, "The people that are with thee are too many for me to give the Midianites into their hands, lest Israel vaunt themselves against me, saying, Mine own hand hath saved me." Verse 12 says, "And the Midianites and the Amalekites and all the children of the east lay along in the valley like grasshoppers for multitude; and their camels were without number, as the sand by the seaside for multitude." These are not good odds for a group of 300 men who each carried only a trumpet, a lamp, and a pitcher.

Who needs warriors and weapons when you have God's walking stick? I would take the Rod any time. We must not fail to comprehend that our greatest weapon and protection against the enemy is the Spirit of God. The odds are against us in this spiritual warfare if we rely solely on our flesh. Remember Romans 8:8, "So then they that are in the flesh cannot please God." We have no power to stand against principalities, evil powers, rulers of this dark world, and spiritual wickedness in high places (Ephesians 6:12). Ours is not a battle of flesh and blood. It is one that demands the Rod. We can only be strong ". . . in the power of his might" (Ephesians 6:10).

We must depend upon the Spirit of God for our protection and defense. Along the rough wilderness terrain of the Middle East, the shepherd's rod was the main tool of defense against wild beasts that threatened the flock. The shepherd would quickly drive them away with a prodding or piercing rod. In Psalm 23:4 we read, "Yea, though I walk through the valley of the shadow of death, I will fear no evil: for thou art with me; thy rod and thy staff they comfort me." What harm can befall us, or what savage devilish imp can overtake us if we hold securely to our Rod? I Peter 5:8-9 warns us to, "Be sober, be vigilant; because your adversary the devil, as a roaring lion, walketh about, seeking whom he may devour. Whom resist steadfast in the faith, knowing that the same afflictions are accomplished (experienced) in your brethren that are in the world."

The day of January 1, 1981, is forever etched in my memory. That is the day that the Rod of the Spirit took me through one of the greatest trials of my life. I had graduated from Liberty Baptist Seminary the previous month and had followed God's call to pastor 35 adults at the Open Door Baptist Church in Tuscaloosa, Alabama. We had been at the church only two Sundays. On the evening of December 31, 1980, we had a wonderful candlelight service that lasted into the New Year. There had been sharing of the Word, testimonies, and much praise and worship. It had been a glorious evening. My wife, Becky, and I were glowing with the light of God on our countenances. God had blessed us immensely by bringing us to Open Door, and we were excited about the ministry he had in store for us there. Our little boy Eric was eight years old. He had been a little trooper all through our seminary years.

Everything seemed wonderful when we went to bed in the early hours of January 1, 1981, after staying up and talking to our wonderful friends Dr. and Mrs. Nevin Alwine. Dr. Alwine had preached the main message of our New Year's Eve service, and he and I had stayed up and talked excitedly about how God was going to use Becky and me to build a great church to capture the city of Tuscaloosa for the Lord. Reluctantly, we went to bed. Early that Thursday morning I was awakened by my precious wife who was having an acute asthma attack. I will never forget it as long as I live. She could not breathe and was gasping for breath. Soon she was as white as a ghost. Having been a paramedic and a police officer prior to being called into the ministry, I immediately knew that she was in grave danger.

I screamed out to Dr. Alwine as I tried to help Becky as she stood at the door trying to get air, "Dr. Alwine, call 911!

Becky is in trouble!" I will never forget the look in her eyes as she pleaded with me, "Help; help me; help me; I can't breathe; I can't breathe; I can't breathe." As she fainted, I caught her and carried her to the couch. As I placed her down, her eyes rolled up into her head, and I knew then that she had gone into cardiac arrest. Her lungs had filled up with fluid. She was literally suffocating to death. Immediately I put her on the floor and began CPR. Dr. Alwine assisted me. An unbelievable amount of fluid kept coming out of her mouth, but I continued to do CPR until the paramedics arrived. They worked with Becky on the floor for about 10 minutes. I kept praying and talking to Dr. Alwine, "No, Lord, don't let my wife die! No, Lord, don't let my wife die! PLEASE, please don't let my wife die, Lord! This can't be happening!"

As the Alwines and I followed the ambulance to the hospital, I will never forget the sick, lonely, helpless feeling that I experienced. Becky was immediately rushed in to the emergency room. We sat in a little waiting room continually crying out to the Lord, "Oh, God, please work." A few men from the church arrived, but I was in shock and was oblivious to my surroundings. As I thought of the possibility of Becky dying, I just kept saying over and over again, "Oh, no God! This can't be happening; this can't be happening!" About an hour later, a doctor asked, "Is Mr. Lovett here?" I said, "I'm Mr. Lovett." I heard the words I had begged God not to hear, "Mr. Lovett, I'm sorry. Your wife is dead." I screamed out, "Oh, no, no! God can't be doing this! This can't be happening! No, no! We just got here. I just graduated from seminary, and my little boy is only 8 years old. No, doctor, this can't be happening. Please, no, no." I was hysterical. The doctor gave me a shot to calm me down, and then they took me back to the apartment.

I will never forget walking into that little bedroom in that apartment and seeing my Bible on the bed. I grabbed it and threw it against the wall and said, "There is no God!" Then I passed out. Hours later I awoke. I was lying across the bed with my face down. The first thing I saw was my Bible lying open. My first inclination was to grab it and tear it apart. But as I reached for it and began to raise it in the air, my attention was drawn to a verse in large, bold letters. It was Romans 8:28, "And we know that all things work together for good to them that love God, to them who are the called according to his purpose." Immediately the Rod of the Spirit began His comforting work. The power of the Holy Spirit through the Word of God literally spoke to my heart and spirit, "Danny, either the will of God is right and good, or it is not. But I promise you it is. And my grace is sufficient, and my strength is made perfect in weakness. That is why you will be able to glory even in this tragedy; because when you are weak, I am strong (II Corinthians 12:9,10).

Immediately I got up and got in the shower. I will never forget standing there with the water running down my face, weeping and asking, "Oh God, why? Why? Why? Why?" Why now, after she had worked so hard to put me through seminary?" The power of the Holy Spirit showed up in that shower and gave me great comfort that morning. The Holy Spirit said to my heart, "Danny, you received the piece of paper, the degree, but Becky received the crown." I came out of that shower shouting. Assurance filled my heart that my wife was with Jesus. She had finished her course, and now it was time for me to ask God to be with me like He had never been with me before.

When a major tragedy strikes your life, you will either get bitter and blame God, or you will get better and become what God wants you to become. We either become a victim or a victor. The way we become the victor is to allow the Rod of the Spirit to comfort and instruct us. Dr. Dan Allender has written in *The Healing Path*:

> "Disruption of shalom is the soil God uses to grow us to become the people we are meant to be. When we are disrupted by illness or death, the goal of spiritual maturity is seldom at the forefront of our thinking nor much comfort in our pain. But God knows that joy—real, succulent pleasure—is being like him. And we will not move to become like him and know the sweet joy he desires for us if we are comfortable where we are. When our peace is shattered, the resulting doubt and confusion send us on a deeply personal search that can transform us and lead us to abundant joy."[1]

My prayer is that your search will lead you to a complete confession of sin and an emptying of self that God might be all to you. Then you will know what it truly means to be controlled by the Rod of the Spirit. You will understand what it means to walk in the Spirit moment-by-moment, day-by-day, giving yourself completely to God that you might manifest the fruit of the Spirit and draw a lost and dying world to Christ.

Seminary training had prepared me for different aspects of church administration. I had been taught courses in theology, leadership, and soul winning—yet, my training had not taught me how to deal with my wife dying in my arms in the first weeks of a new ministry. Only the Rod of the Spirit could take me through that tragedy. In

Gideon's case it was the Rod that brought fire out of the rock. Gideon took a deployment of troops with strange objects in their hands, but it was the Rod that wrought the victory.

We in America must get back to faith in the living God and hold onto the Rod of the Spirit. II Corinthians 5:7 say, "For we walk by faith, not by sight." In II Kings 19:14 we read that when Hezekiah, king of Israel, received the threat of war from the Assyrian army, he went into the house of the Lord, spread the threatening letter out before the Lord, and then prayed. Would to God that we would do that in America today! Thank God for our defense program and our strong armies. We must realize, however, that above everything else, we must rely on our Rod to take us through every trial that we face.

Let us now turn our attention to David, first mentioned in the Old Testament as a lowly young shepherd boy. He was the eighth and youngest son of Jesse. In I Samuel 17, we find the story of Goliath, the Philistine, that giant of a man who tormented the Israelite armies. At his father's instruction, David had gone to check on his three oldest brothers and take them food supplies. They were members of Saul's army. When David arrived at their camp, he heard Goliath's challenge and saw the reproach that this man was bringing on Israel in his defiance of the armies of the living God.

When the men of Israel saw Goliath, they ran in fear away from him. David, however, spoke boldly and asked, "Who is this uncircumcised Philistine, that he should defy the armies of the living God?" (I Samuel 17:26) He volunteered to go alone against the blasphemous giant. Of course, David's older brothers were angry when they heard David say this. I would paraphrase their sarcastic remarks as, "David, what are you doing around here anyway? Who did you leave with your few little sheep? You just wanted to see the battle, you cocky little brat. You're no soldier." When Saul, the king of Israel, heard of David's offer, he sent for him. He was desperately willing to try anything. David testified that he knew that God was with him and that God would empower him to silence the belligerent enemy of Israel. In verse 37 David said, "The LORD that delivered me out of the paw of the lion, and out of the paw of the bear, he will deliver me out of the hand of this Philistine. And Saul said unto David, Go, and the LORD be with thee."

David was convinced that all God needed was a willing vessel. Saul was certainly not as convinced of the power of God as was David. He tried to arm David by placing his armor and helmet on the young boy, loading him down with the essentials for battle—armor, shield, helmet, and a sword. This is the paraphernalia that the world deems necessary. I especially like what David said in verse 39 when he removed the armor after a few steps with it on. In essence he said, "I can't move with this stuff on." Verse 40 says, "And he took his staff in his hand, and chose him five smooth stones out of the brook, and put them in a shepherd's bag which he had, even in a scrip; and his sling was in his hand: and he drew near to the Philistine."

When Goliath looked at David he could not believe his eyes. He must have thought to himself, "Why, this is just a little, red-cheeked, snotty-nosed kid!" I am amused when I read the Philistine's response in verse 43, "Am I a dog, that thou comest to me with staves? And the Philistine cursed David by his gods." In other words, "What do you think you're coming out here to kill a dog? All you have is a slingshot and that slippery little stick in your hand." What the giant did not know was that that stick was more than an ordinary stave. It was the Rod of the Spirit; representing the power and presence of an awesome, almighty God Who rules the universe.

David responded to Goliath with these words, "Thou comest to me with a sword, and with a spear, and with a shield: but I come to thee in the name of the LORD of hosts, the God of the armies of Israel, whom thou hast defied. This day will the LORD deliver thee into mine hand; and I will smite thee, and take thine head from thee; and I will give the carcasses of the host of the Philistines this day unto the fowls of the air, and to the wild beasts of the earth; that all the earth may know that there is a God in Israel. And all this assembly shall know that the LORD saveth not with sword and spear: for the battle is the LORD'S, and he will give you into our hands." That very day the Philistines knew that there was a God in heaven, for Goliath had met his match. One small stone from David's sling went straight into Goliath's forehead. David had smote the Philistine! The world's champion was dead! We must never forget that nothing is impossible with God. God's Rod will always take us through our trials, our tragedies, and our battles.

There are many Biblical examples of mighty men of valor and their heroic deeds. David's mighty men have especially fascinated me. Adino, the chief of the captains, lifted up his spear against 800 strong men at one time and slew them all. Eleazar, the son of Dodo, rose up and smote the Philistines until his hand had adhered to his sword. Once, under Philistine attack, all Shammah's men deserted him. He stood in the middle of a field all by himself, beat back the Philistines, and God gave him a great victory.

Another mighty man of valor is Benaiah. In II Samuel 23:21 and in I Chronicles 11:23-24 we read the story of how he killed an Egyptian warrior who was seven and one-half feet tall. The Egyptian had a thick spear in his hand, but Benaiah went down to him with his staff (his rod), plucked the spear out of the Egyptian's hand and slew him with his own spear. What a contrast! One combats an army with a spear the size of a weaver's beam, the other, a rod the size of a broom handle. That is like going after a grizzly bear with a hickory stick! I prefer the hickory stick with the power of God. Remember Ephesians 3:20, "Now unto him that is able to do exceeding abundantly above all that we ask or think, according to the power that worketh in us."

One of the most delightful scriptures that emphasizes the blessings of God upon His people is found in Numbers 13:17-25. I love to preach from this passage and dramatize how the twelve spies were sent from the wilderness of the land to spy out the land of Canaan. They were instructed to go up into the mountain to see what God had prepared for them. They were allowed a foretaste of the good things that were waiting for them on the other side of Jordan. Not only did they see the land and its plentiful fruit, but they could get a glimpse of their opposition as well. They realized they had to drive out the inhabitants of Canaan and overthrow the city's stronghold. The result would be a multitude of God's blessings upon them. Numbers 13:18-20 states, "And see the land, what it is, and the people that dwelleth therein, whether they be strong or weak, few or many; And what the land is that they dwell in, whether it be good or bad; and what cities they be that they dwell in, whether in tents, or in strongholds; And what the land is, whether it be fat or lean, whether there be wood therein, or not. And be ye of good courage, and bring of the fruit of the land. Now the time was the time of the first ripe grapes."

I believe Canaan is an example of the type of dwelling

place that God has for all believers. It is a land of abundant life where the spiritual air is pure, refreshing waters flow, and the fruit of blessings abound. A land that flows with milk and honey, Canaan is the land of abundant, spirit-filled living. Every believer should desire to dwell there. It is a place of spiritual victory where the enemy is defeated in daily conquest. This does not mean that there are no giants there. There are great walls of the city that must be marched around, and there are mountains to climb. As we submit to our Joshua (Jesus), however, we will be more than conquerors. Jesus said in John 10:10, "I am come that they might have life, and that they might have it more abundantly."

As a believer and rightful heir, have you visited this land, tasted of the fruit therein and viewed the beautiful green valley from Mt. Pisgah's lofty heights? Have you drunk from the refreshing springs of Nagev and felt a surge of spiritual power? I wish I could say that I have personally found a permanent rest there and have experienced all that God intends for believers to enjoy. But I can honestly say I have been there. I thank God for that and pray that by His grace, He will continue to enable me to present to others a taste of that blessed fruit of Canaan.

When Moses sent the spies into Canaan it was the time of the first harvesting of grapes. Numbers 13:23 tells us, "And they came unto the brook of Eshcol, and cut down from thence a branch with one cluster of grapes, and they bare it between two upon a staff." Can you imagine the joy and delight to be invited to enter the camp? If the grapes were the size of apples, can you imagine how big the tomatoes, oranges, cantaloupes, and melons must have been? I would love to have seen the Israelites eyes when they beheld such a wonder. Are we amazed and filled with excitement and wonder when we think about the fruit of the Spirit? It thrills me to think of what God has in store for all of His children who enter into the abundant land of the Spirit-filled life!

When the apostle Paul described Christian character in Galatians 5:23-26, he used an analogy calling it the fruit of the Spirit. Stand with me in awe as Paul displays each magnificent cluster of fruit! These fruits include: love, joy, peace, longsuffering, gentleness, goodness, faith, meekness and self-control. Each big cluster of fruit is born on a rod or staff, the Holy Spirit. As the grapes of Eschol were borne on a staff between two men, so also is the fruit of abundant Christian character borne on the staff of the Spirit, the Rod of the Spirit. The flesh can never bear the load of the fruit as described in Galatians 5. It is an impossible task in one's own effort. Man in the flesh simply cannot sustain such a burden. Without the Rod, we are incapable of carrying the fruit of Canaan back for others to view. In Galatians 5:16 Paul said, "Walk in the Spirit, and ye shall not fulfill the lust of the flesh."

After 40 days of searching out the land, the spies returned and showed the fruit of the land to Moses, Aaron, and the children of Israel. They agreed that Canaan was a land flowing with milk and honey, but then they said, "Nevertheless . . ." they wanted blessings without battles, mountains without valleys, and rainbows without rainstorms. "Nevertheless," they said, "the people be strong that dwell in the land, and the cities are walled, and very great: and moreover we saw the children of Anak (giants) there" (Numbers 13:28). Just as many Christians do today, they were negative and made excuses for refusing to believe God.

Caleb refused to believe the negative report. He encouraged the people that they should go up at once and possess the land because they were well able to conquer it. Caleb was saying, in essence, that the rod, which carried the blessing of the giant fruit, would also carry the giant men away from them. He reassured the people and prompted them to continue to trust the Rod. God always finished what He begins. Nothing is ever too hard for Him. We must trust our precious Rod to give us victory in every situation as He safely carries us through trials. Psalm 46:1 promises, "God is our refuge and strength, a very present help in trouble." Because of fear and unbelief, there are many who will never enter the Promised Land that flows with milk and honey.

Numbers 14:1-2 records the response of the children of Israel to Caleb's good report, "And all the congregation lifted up their voice, and cried; and the people wept that night. And all the children of Israel murmured against Moses and against Aaron: and the whole congregation said unto them, 'Would God that we had died in the land of Egypt! or would God we had died in this wilderness!'" As a consequence of their continual griping against God and Moses, they spent the next 40 years wandering in the desolate wilderness where they did indeed die. God punished Israel one year of toil for every day the spies viewed the good things of Canaan. The spies had beheld the beauty of Canaan for 40 days, and now they would view the ugly desolation of the wilderness for 40 years. They paid a terrible price for unbelief and murmuring. It was costly to choose gripes instead of grapes.

The price for the rejection of God's anointing is no less today. I am horrified by the unbelief and murmuring heard today against God and God's men when the command of Christ is to walk forth in the victorious life of the Spirit. Christians seem very content to wander in the desert lands of sin and self, continually murmuring about wanting the leaks and onions of Egypt. There will never be power in service or victory over sin until Christians today are willing to exercise the same kind of leadership that was demonstrated by Caleb and Joshua. They were the only two individuals of the entire generation who had faith and trust in God to trust Him to take them over into the blessed land of spiritual Canaan. Are you camping in Canaan's land, or are you teetering between the land of grapes and gripes? Let us never forget the words of Jesus in John 6:43, "Murmur not among yourselves." Allow the Rod of the Spirit to control and direct you, and you will walk victoriously through any trial and tragedy that comes your way.

After my wife Becky went to be with Jesus, God brought Susan, my present wife, into my life. One Wednesday night when Susan was five and one-half months pregnant with our second child, I was getting ready to preach at my church when George Baugh, our chairman of deacons, ran to the pulpit. He said anxiously, "Danny, you've got to come quickly; they have just taken Susan to the hospital. She is having severe pains with the baby." As I walked into the hospital, they immediately took me to Susan's room. Dr Harvey Edwards was there. He told me they had given Susan medication to stop the labor, and then he said these words that I will never forget, "Danny, we must stop this labor. If we do not, the baby will be born. And the tragedy is—he will be born dead." I said, "Oh, Dr. Harvey, whatever you do, please stop this labor." What a joy to have a Christian doctor who then said, "Let's pray."

As the evening wore on, I sat and prayed while Susan drifted in and out of sleep due to the drugs. At one point I looked at Dr. Edwards and saw that he had tears in his eyes. He turned and said to me, "Brother Danny, I'm sorry; I can't stop this labor. The baby is going to be born soon, within an hour. He will be dead." I'll never forget what I said, "Oh, no, Dr. Edwards, please, please do something. What can we do? Please!" But there was nothing we could do. I fell across Susan's chest and wept, "Honey I'm sorry. I'm sorry." While I heaved with sobs, she put her arms around me, rubbed my head and said, "Honey, it's okay. The Lord giveth and the Lord taketh away. Blessed be the name of the Lord." And like Job, she did not charge God foolishly. I remember sitting there and praying after that and watching the monitor. It had been making a beeping sound, but soon the sound started to decrease until there was straight line and a continuous eerie rumble. I knew my little boy was dead. That was a giant in my life. Dr. Edwards asked, "What do you want me to do with your little boy?" I said, "Put him in my hands." He filled my hands with his completely developed little body.

As I sat there and held that little boy, I remembered how five and one-half years earlier Becky had died in my arms. The same sweet Spirit who showed up in the shower that day, revealed Himself to me as I sat holding my little boy. The Rod of the Spirit gave me a peace that passes all understanding. As I looked up as if toward heaven, I asked, "Lord, what about my little boy?" I will never forget the peace that came with the confirmation that was given to me that night through the power of the Rod of the Spirit, the Holy Spirit. It was as if God said, "Remember five and one-half years ago when I took your wife? She is here with me now. Just as I sent Susan to you to take care of Eric, you don't have to worry about your little boy because Becky is taking care of him." I came up out of that chair greatly excited, wrapped in the warm fact that my precious Lord has everything under control. I felt strengthened to do a funeral that was scheduled for the next morning.

For years, we had prayed for the husband of a woman in our church to get saved, and God had gloriously answered our prayers. Johnny had been saved only three weeks when a car he was working on fell on him, crushing and killing him. We knew there would be many lost people at the funeral. The morning after my little boy died, God enabled me to get up and go preach that funeral. While at the hospital before leaving for the funeral, I was met by a counselor who had been sent to Susan's room. "Are you Mr. Lovett?" she asked. "I am here to console you." I looked at her and said, "Excuse me, Ma'am but I don't need to be consoled. I have the Comforter, God the Holy Spirit consoling me. This is the day the Lord has made, and I am going to rejoice and be glad in it. Let me explain something to you. Five and one-half years ago I was married to a lady named Becky. She died and is now in heaven. Then God gave me Susan, and last night Susan delivered our little boy who was born dead. But our little boy is in heaven. I know that because in the Old Testament of the Bible we read about David who had a little boy who died also. After David's boy died, David looked up and said, 'I know he can't come to me, but I can go to him.' So, I know my little boy is in heaven, and an exciting thing I know is that my wife Becky is now taking care of him! So you don't have to worry about me because I am happy. By the way, I have to go now to conduct a funeral."

That counselor must have surely thought, "This man is traumatized. He has lost it!" I left that day and preached the gospel at that Johnny's funeral. God's grace is always sufficient; His strength is made perfect in our weakness. "Most gladly therefore will I rather glory in my infirmities, that the power of Christ may rest upon me" (2 Corinthians 12:9). The Holy Spirit, the Rod of the Spirit, was with me every step and in every word that I spoke. At the conclusion of that funeral sermon, 24 people came to know Jesus Christ as their personal Savior. How could I have preached that service? It was because the Rod of the Spirit conquered my giant.

The last illustration I want to use about the power of the rod is probably the most important one in the Old Testament, and that involves Aaron's rod. Aaron was chosen by God to accompany Moses and minister as his aid. During the exodus and wilderness wanderings we read of the continual complaining and murmuring of the children of Israel against both Moses and Aaron. There are always people who murmur against God's chosen men. Jesus said in Luke 6:26, "Woe unto you, when all men shall speak well of you! For so did their fathers to the false prophets."

Sadly, murmuring and complaining are all too familiar in the body of Christ. I believe that the deadly, evil sin of murmuring is an enormous problem plaguing the church today. The Israelites complained about everything. Nothing seemed to satisfy them. They griped when their needs were not met, as well as when they were. Their complaints were endless. They despised their leaders and longed to be back in Egypt. Numbers 11:1 tells us, "And when the people complained, it displeased the LORD: and the LORD heard it; and His anger was kindled; and the fire of the LORD burnt among them, and consumed them that were in the uttermost parts of the camp."

A visible sign of a Christian who is out of fellowship with the Lord is a complaining spirit. The greatest grief to the Lord is the complaining and murmuring against the men of God whom he has called and anointed as leaders. In Numbers 16, we read the story of the rebellion of Korah and about 350 men. This group rose up against Moses and Aaron's leadership saying, "Ye take too much upon you, seeing all the congregation are holy, every one of them, and the LORD is among them: wherefore then lift ye up yourselves above the congregation of the LORD? (3). Korah challenged Moses and Aaron's leadership before the whole congregation. When Moses heard Korah's words, he fell upon his face. God vindicated his leadership after he spoke to the people when, ". . . the ground clave asunder that was under them: And the earth opened her mouth, and swallowed them up, and their houses, and all the men that appertained unto Korah, and all their goods. They, and all that appertained to them, went down alive into the pit, and the earth closed upon them: and they perished from among the congregation." The remaining Israelites, realizing God's wrath, confessed their sins against God's anointed.

In order to avoid the necessity of ever having to repeat such a drastic measure, God chose another way of manifesting his favor upon his chosen leader. God often has a unique and unusual way of choosing those whom he calls to minister in the temple. God wanted there to be no question as to His selection of High Priest over Israel, so He ordained a special sign that would rest upon His anointed. He instructed each of the 12 tribes of Israel to engrave their name upon a rod and bring it to the tabernacle of the congregation. The Lord told Moses, "And it shall come to pass, that the man's rod, whom I shall choose, shall blossom: and I will make to cease from me the murmurings of the children of Israel, whereby they murmur against you" (Numbers 17:5).

My firm belief is that the rods that were brought to Moses were not freshly cut sticks, but dead, dry sage or staff, empty of sap and lifeless. I believe they were the personal staffs that each tribal leader carried with him out of Egypt. The day after the rods were assembled in the Tabernacle, Moses found that Aaron's rod ". . . was budded, and brought forth buds, and bloomed blossoms, and yielded almonds" (Numbers 17:8). God had chosen Aaron. His rod could not be mistaken as a fraud. The Lord then instructed Moses, "Bring Aaron's rod again before the testimony, to be kept for a token against the rebels; and thou shalt quite take away their murmurings from me, that they die not."

The proof of God's anointing on an individual today is evident by the fact that what He accomplishes cannot be performed by the flesh, by physical strength, but only by the presence of the supernatural. It is impossible for the natural man to produce bud, blossom, and fruit all at once. Many ministries today are empowered by man's expertise and abilities but fail to manifest the supernatural, miracle-working power of the Holy Spirit. When a man of God stands before a congregation, the supernatural power of God will be evident in his life. He will teach and preach with God's authority, in the power of the Spirit (I Corinthians 2:13). Aaron's ministry is distinguishable from others in that it manifested the blessings of God and yielded a God-given increase.

I believe that there are too many men in the ministry today who are clutching dry, dead, lifeless rods. There are no signs of fruitfulness or productivity in their ministry. Many of them are self-called, self-motivated, and self-empowered preachers. They preach dead sermons to dead congregations. There is no function of the Holy Spirit. The absence of tears of compassion, fiery sermons, and budding rods are indicators of the deadness of which I speak. There are some who would have you believe that the anointing of

God is on their life. They temporarily bud forth, but there are no genuine blossoms and no lasting fruit. Jesus said in John 15:5, 16, "I am the vine, ye are the branches. He that abideth in me, and I in him, the same bringeth forth much fruit; for without me ye can do nothing. Ye have not chosen me, but I have chosen you, and ordained you, that ye should go and bring forth fruit, and that your fruit should remain; that whatsoever ye shall ask of the Father in my name, he may give it you."

The fruitfulness of life in the Rod constitutes anointing for service. We saw that Aaron's rod budded, blossomed, and yielded almonds. Notice that Scripture does not tell us how many buds blossomed or how many almonds there were. Numbers do not mean anointing. Size does not constitute success. Assets do not indicate anointing. The complexity of the operation does not validate one's calling. God's anointing on a man's life is not measured by a fleet of buses, a congregation of several thousand, radio and television programs, the kind of car he drives, or the architecture of his church building.

We must not be deceived by numbers or size because great things can be accomplished in the flesh.

Aaron's rod ". . .brought forth buds, and bloomed blossoms, and yielded almonds" (Numbers 17:8). Buds symbolize life. It is the Spirit who gives life. The flesh profits nothing (John 6:63). Paul said in II Corinthians 3:6, "Who also hath made us able ministers of the new testament; not of the letter, but of the spirit: for the letter killeth, but the spirit giveth life." When I look at trees in the springtime, especially the apple trees next to my home, I see old, dry, brown limbs and sticks that seem dead or lifeless. The first sign of life comes when buds break forth upon the branches of those apple trees. Likewise, the first sign of God's anointing in new life manifests itself in an outward bud. The Bible says, those who look to him are radiant and shall never be ashamed (Psalm 34:5). II Corinthians 3:18 declares, "But we all, with open face, beholding as in a glass the glory of the Lord, are changed into the same image from glory to glory, even as by the Spirit of the Lord." To the preacher I would ask, "Is there life in your ministry? Does your preaching generate enthusiasm, joy, newness, and an outward expression of life in your congregation?" The Bible says, "But ye are a chosen generation, a royal priesthood, an holy nation, a peculiar people; that ye should show forth the praises of him who hath called you out of darkness into his marvelous light" (I Peter 2:9).

Blossoms symbolize sweet fragrance. I love the smell of springtime in the air in Lynchburg near our apple orchard. The air is permeated with the smell of apple blossoms, an unmistakable sign of spring. Our ministries must bear the fragrance of the Holy Spirit. God said, "And I will put my spirit within you, and cause you to walk in my statutes, and ye shall keep my judgments, and do them" (Ezekiel 36:27). To stay true to Christ and be that sweet-smelling fragrance, we must follow His Word and His Spirit. As Christ lives and abides in us, and as we are continuously filled with the Holy Spirit, our lives will overflow with the fragrance of Christ. The saved and the unsaved alike will be drawn to us, "For we are unto God a sweet savor of Christ, in them that are saved, and in them that perish" (II Corinthians 2:15).

Fruit symbolizes the final product. Aaron's rod bore fruit. Jesus said in Matthew 7:20, "Wherefore by their fruits ye shall know them." To the pastor, people are the product of his ministry. The pastor sets the spiritual level of his church, and the fruit of his labors will not only be the conversion of souls but also the maturity and spiritual development of the body of Christ. His laborers may not be in great volume, but his work will manifest life, freshness, and the character of God in his flock. God is not impressed with explosive, flamboyant beginnings, but with lasting, eternal, results.

Some of the most precious men of God whom I know labor faithfully in small churches with ministries that are fruitful, edifying, and nurturing. There is joy and peace among their flock. They have a feeling of contentment because they are well fed. The flock is not complacent, nor do they speak against the shepherd. The pastor demonstrates the character of Christ as he lovingly and firmly feeds, comforts, and disciples his flock. He is an example of a soul winner and manifests the fruit of the Holy Spirit. The evidence of the anointing of God upon his life is not found in his talent or ability, nor in his education or methods of administration. It is evident when he demonstrates to his people that God is supernaturally at work in his life, ever bearing spiritual fruit for God's glory.

I would like to make one final point regarding Aaron and his budding rod. As God gave specific instructions to Moses to build the tabernacle in the wilderness, he instructed him to place three items inside the Ark of the Covenant. These three items were to remain there as a token for all generations. In Hebrews 9:3-4 there is a listing of these three items, "And after the second veil, the tabernacle which is called the Holiest of all; Which had the golden censer, and the ark of the covenant overlaid round about with gold, wherein was the golden pot that had manna, and Aaron's rod that budded, and the tables of the covenant."

It is not surprising to me that God would choose to place the rod of Aaron in such a holy place. The tables of the covenant, or the tables of stone, the Ten

Commandments, typify the Father as the Lawgiver. The golden pot of manna typifies Jesus Christ as the Bread of Life. It seems entirely appropriate and fitting to complete the representation of the Trinity with Aaron's budded rod, typifying the precious Third Person of the Godhead, the Holy Spirit. The Ark of the Covenant, which was placed behind the second veil in the Holy of Holies, is a picture of our triune God dwelling among His people.

If God did not exclude the Holy Spirit from the Holy of Holies, let us not exclude Him from our lives and from our ministries. The Savior's word to his disciples still applies today, "Behold, I send the promise of my Father upon you: but tarry ye in the city of Jerusalem, until ye be endued with power from on high" (Luke 24:49). It is not a repetition of Pentecost that we need but rather the realization that Pentecost has never ended. Let us be continually reminded that the Spirit of God lives within us. If you desperately long for His power to be manifest in your life, there are no boundaries to what God will do in and through your life.

CHAPTER 7

THE CHOSEN VESSEL

**"But we have this treasure in earthen vessels, that the
excellency of the power may be of God and not of us."
II Corinthians 4:7**

The Lord delights in using a life of weakness that is considered of little use to the world. I place myself in this category. When people looked at me when I was a teenager, they saw outward signs of weakness, inadequacy, and insecurity. They could not see that deep down in the heart of this poor, country boy God was building a mighty faith and stirring an unquenchable fire. Because they so aptly express part of my life story, Paul's words in I Corinthians 1:26-31 are dear to me:

> "For ye see your calling, brethren, how
> that not many wise men after the flesh, not
> many mighty, not many noble, are called:
> But God hath chosen the foolish things

of the world to confound the wise; and God
hath chosen the weak things of the world to
confound the things which are mighty; And
base things of the world, and things which
are despised, hath God chosen, yea, and
things which are not, to bring to nought
things that are: That no flesh should glory
in his presence. But of Him are ye in Christ
Jesus, who of God is made unto us wisdom,
and righteousness, and sanctification, and
redemption: That, according as it is written,
'He that glorieth, let him glory in the Lord.'"

God is the source of our relationship with Christ (30).
That relationship is a personal and living relationship. The
verses just quoted indicate that our union and identification with Christ result in our possessing God's wisdom
(Colossians 2:3); our right standing with God (2
Corinthians 5:21); our sanctification (I Thessalonians 4:3-
7); and our penalty having been paid by Christ Jesus (Mark
10:45). As we walk with the Rod of the Spirit as His chosen
vessel, we allow these truths to shape our lives.

As I look back at my life, I see how I came to God with
feebleness and uncertainty. In His infinite grace, He began
to mold and shape me, working in my life to produce confidence and maturity. What He did in my life He can do in
the life of every empty, broken vessel. I am reminded of a
Scripture passage in Jeremiah 18:2-4:

"'Arise, and go down to the potter's
house, and there I will cause thee to hear
my words.' Then I went down to the potter's house, and behold, he wrought a work
on the wheels. And the vessel that he made

of clay was marred in the hand of the potter: so he made it again another vessel, as seemed good to the potter to make it."

At times God must break a vessel before He can use it. We may think we are an irreparable vessel, but God takes the soft clay, remakes it, and shapes it into a vessel of His choosing. The Lord can make us into a useful vessel when we submit our will, ambitions, strength, skill, talent, and knowledge to Him. Isaiah 64:8 says, "But now, O LORD, thou art our Father; we are the clay, and thou our potter; and we all are the work of thy hand." Paul asked in Romans 9:21, "Hath not the potter power over the clay, of the same lump to make one vessel unto honor, and another unto dishonor?" Paul was not saying that some people are worth more than others; He was simply implying that the Creator has control over the created object. The created object or created person therefore has no right to demand anything from God. His very existence depends upon the Lord.

When you and I keep the perspective that we are created by God for His pleasure, with differing gifts and abilities that He has given us, we then have no room for pride and personal agendas. That is why Paul said that we are not sufficient in ourselves, but our sufficiency is of God, (II Corinthians 3:5). When God found me, He found a shattered vessel with little potential. From a human perspective, no one thought I would ever amount to anything worthwhile. God delights in finding a vessel that is broken and willing to place itself in the hands of the Master. Broken over great sin, the Psalmist David wrote, "The sacrifices of God are a broken spirit: a broken and a contrite heart, O God, thou wilt not despise" (Psalm 51:17). We can never please God or earn His favor through good deeds.

God looks for a heart attitude of genuine remorse and repentance over our sin. This humility pleases Him. "Humble yourselves therefore under the mighty hand of God, that he may exalt you in due time" (II Peter 5:6).

In John 6 we read the story of a hungry multitude. When Jesus questioned Philip about feeding them, Philip replied, "Two hundred pennyworth of bread is not sufficient for them, that every one of them may take a little" (7). Andrew then pointed out that there was a young lad in the crowd who had five barley loaves and two small fish, but he asked, ". . . but what are they among so many?' (9). The young lad then gave what he had to Jesus, as inadequate and insufficient as it seemed, and Jesus multiplied and fed five thousand people that day. The lad gave all Jesus needed because it was presented to Him in faith.

The little lad was willing to pick up the Rod of the Spirit and walk with Him. This story shows us the divine intention of Jesus to take an unknown boy and bless not only multitudes by the Sea of Galilee but countless others throughout the centuries. The story of this young boy who gave all he had, gives this miracle relevance for your life and mine. God desires that we yield our bodies to the Lord Jesus Christ and allow the Holy Spirit to fill us. That is what it really means to walk with the Rod of the Spirit. Just like the lad in John 6, you and I, as chosen vessels of the Lord, are asked to pick up the rod and be available to God.

Let us notice four aspects about the young lad's attitude. First, he sought Jesus. The story did not tell us what influenced this boy to follow the crowd in order to see Jesus. He may have had godly parents who encouraged him to seek the Master. On the other hand, he may have heard of some wonderful miracles the Savior had performed, and so followed the multitude in hopes of witnessing to others.

This is just mere speculation, but I think that he got up that morning with a tender heart's yearning and longing to see Jesus. Perhaps his parents were excited because their son wanted to see the Master. His mother, being a godly mother thrilled with her son's desire, fixed him a little lunch. They were poor people, as evidenced by the barley bread and two small fish. Maybe his mother told him to share his meal if others were hungry. We don't really know. What is clear is that the boy was there just when Jesus needed him. There was willingness in his heart to seek the Lord. No one seeks Jesus in this fashion without finding Him. Jeremiah 29:13 tells us, "And ye shall seek me, and find me, when ye shall search for me with all your heart."

Jesus came into the world seeking to save that which was lost (Luke 19:10). When a seeking Savior meets a seeking sinner, it is the moment of truth. If you are seeking Jesus then you are a candidate for blessings. When you are seeking Jesus, you are walking with the Rod. Listen to Andrew Murray, a man who was filled with the Holy Spirit and lived a life of absolute surrender to God:

> "A man who is separated unto the Holy Ghost is a man who is given up to say: 'Father, let the Holy Ghost have full dominion over me, in my home, in my temper, in every word of my tongue, in every thought of my heart, in every feeling toward my fellow men; let the Holy Spirit have entire possession.' Is that what has been the longing and the covenant of your heart with your God— to be a man or a woman separated and given up unto the Holy Ghost? I pray you listen to the voice of Heaven. 'Separate me,' said the Holy Ghost. Yes, separated unto the Holy

Ghost. May God grant that the Word may enter into the very depths of our being to search us, and if we discover that we have not come out from the world entirely, if God discovers to us that the self-life, self-will, self-exaltation are there, let us humble ourselves before Him."

The second aspect about the lad's attitude that we want to consider is his willingness to serve Jesus. It is evident from the story that he thought so much of Christ that when he was asked to part with his five loaves and two small fish, he was ready to surrender them. When you and I are walking with the Rod, the Holy Spirit, we willingly surrender all that we are and have to the Master for His use. God is worthy of our total surrender, without it He cannot work to completely carry out his plan and purpose for our lives.

Let us look thirdly at the lad's potential. He gave Jesus everything he had, which was really not much. Those five barley loaves represent the lowest food staple in any Jewish home. Barley loaves were usually given to donkeys, mules, and other livestock. Only the destitute ate barley loaves; the standard loaves were made of wheat. The two small fish, probably caught in the Sea of Galilee, were evidently cooked and probably quite shriveled up. The boy gave all he had, and what potential it was in the hands of the Master! How true are the quaint words we hear so often, "Little is much when God is in it." The poor lad offered his all, his meager meal, and it was enough to fulfill the will of the Master.

In this story of the lad and his little lunch we see the potential of supplying the need of thousands of hungry people. Counting the women and children, the little boy's loaves and fish probably fed and satisfied approximately 20,000 people. God delights to do the miraculous when he finds a life totally sold out to Him. Total surrender is a work of the Holy Spirit. God sees our heart's desire. When He finds a man or woman who desperately longs for the powerful infilling of the Holy Spirit, God will move in that life ". . . both to will (choose) and to do of his good pleasure" (Philippians 2:13). A natural by-product of walking with the Rod of the Spirit will be a life that blesses and meets the needs of multitudes of people.

The command of our Savior is to "Go ye into all the world, and preach the gospel to every creature" (Mark 16:15). This is not figurative language. Jesus was not using rhetoric. He meant exactly what He said, "*all* the world . . . to *every* creature." The disciples took these words so seriously that the then-known world was evangelized in thirty years after the day of Pentecost. The basic need of men and women today is still the saving knowledge of the Lord Jesus Christ. There is no duty we can render that has more importance or urgency than that of sharing the Bread of Life with lost humanity. May we respond as the little lad who gave his all in service to the Master.

A fourth aspect of the lad is his responsibility. The Lord Jesus would never have accepted the loaves and fish from the boy unless there had been some level of mature responsibility in the lad's heart. He was a youth confronted with a responsible moment, an extremely defining moment in his life. When Andrew pointed him out, the lad knew that he could be of service. He was not slow to present what he had and make it available to Christ. Responsibility has been defined as our response to God's ability. Somehow this lad knew that, in the hands of the Savior, his little parcel of food could be sanctified and multiplied. As soon as Andrew brought him to the Savior, the young boy acted with consuming responsibility and yielded his all to the Savior.

Jesus took the loaves and fish, gave thanks, and then distributed them to the disciples (John 6:11). Notice that the loaves and the fish did not change or multiply at that particular moment. The emphasis here is on the willingness of Christ to accept the five small loaves and two small fish. What a glorious lesson this is for all of us! Jesus Christ takes what we give Him no matter how small our contribution might seem. Once our all is in His hands—our gifts, talents, abilities—He sanctifies them by the power of cleansing life and love. We cannot read this story and have an excuse for holding back our five loaves and two small fish. We may sense our unworthiness and utter sinfulness, but if we are prepared to yield our all to Jesus, He will accept us and use us. Paul appealed to Christians, "I beseech you therefore, brethren, by the mercies of God, that ye present your bodies a living sacrifice, holy, acceptable unto God, which is your reasonable service. And be not conformed to this world: but be ye transformed by the renewing of your mind, that ye may prove what is that good, and acceptable, and perfect will of God" (Romans 12:1-2).

The lad trusted all to the Savior, and his offering met the need of thousands. By His creative power, the Lord of all life compressed into a moment of time what naturally takes months. This is the essence of a miracle. Miracles require faith. It takes no imagination to realize that the boy was aware that the Savior was about to feed a multitude with his lunch. Yet, without hesitation, he yielded and trusted his all to Christ. God honored that simple faith and hungry people were fed to overflowing. I like to image the little boy sitting and watching as Jesus took his lunch and fed thousands. His eyes must have been wide with amazement and his heart full of gratitude that he, an unknown poor lad, had been allowed to be part of a miracle! If you and I will walk with the Rod of the Spirit, we too can be greatly used by God. All God asks is for your availability, your potential, and your responsibility in giving Him your all. As we do our part, God will do the rest, and the world will be blessed.

I will never forget the day we left Sylvester, Georgia, with everything that we owned. My wife, Becky, our three-year-old son, Eric, and I packed a U-Haul truck and set out to obey God. I felt very much like the young lad who gave his lunch to Jesus. I said, "Lord, I don't have much to give, but please take our all. We are insufficient, but we give everything to You." Praise God! What happened in the next few years is nothing short of miraculous. God made provision for every need. I can truly say today that God has used my life to minister to thousands who are hungry and thirsty for the truth. Through God's power in my life and His miracle of multiplying the little things, He has used my family and me to touch many lives for Christ. God used us at the Open Door Baptist Church in Tuscaloosa, Alabama, and now he is using us here at Liberty University. I give God all the praise and glory. Everything that has been accomplished in my life and ministry is due to the Rod that God placed in my hand. In the flesh I can do nothing, but in the Spirit I can do all things.

The Lord spoke to the great prophet Elijah when he was hiding in a cave, discouraged and alone. God told Elijah to leave the cave and obey his commands.

I Kings 19:19-20 tells us:

"So he departed thence, and found Elisha

the son of Shaphat, who was plowing with
twelve yoke of oxen before him, and he with
the twelfth: and Elijah passed by him, and
cast his mantle upon him. And he left the
oxen, and ran after Elijah, and said, Let me, I
pray thee, kiss my father and my mother, and
then I will follow thee. And he said unto
him, Go back again: for what have I done to
thee?"

Elisha started with nothing. He prayed for a double
portion of Elijah's spirit, and God answered his prayer.
Scripture tells us that after God took Elijah to heaven in a
chariot of fire, Elisha took his mantle and stood by the
banks of the Jordan River. The rod of Elijah was now in the
hands of Elisha. II Kings 2:14 tells us what happened, "And
he took the mantle of Elijah that fell from him, and smote
the waters, and said, Where is the LORD God of Elijah?
And when he also had smitten the waters, they parted hith-
er and thither: and Elisha went over." Let us pray today as
we walk with the Rod of the Spirit that God will allow us a
double portion of His Spirit as we seek to carry the gospel
to the world.

It is very interesting to study the lives of Elijah and
Elisha and to compare the miracles that God performed
through each man. God used Elisha to perform approximately twice as many miracles through his ministry as that
of Elijah's. First and II Kings contain at least twice as many
written pages to record the exploits of Elisha as compared
to the life of Elijah. Elisha truly received a double portion
of Elijah's Spirit. The beautiful truth is obvious. God is not
only looking for available vessels who are willing to be filled
with His Spirit, but He is looking for those who wish a

double filling that they might bring glory to His name.

God will fill every space in your life and mine that we submit to Him. Our lives and our ministries fail only because we fail to offer to God our all. God is only as big in your life and mine as the space we give Him to possess. I have heard people say that in order to be filled with the Spirit we need more of the Lord. I disagree. We can have no more of God than what we now possess; rather, He needs more of us. God has already given His all to us; it is we who need to give our all to Him. Perhaps we would have room for the Spirit of God if we would empty our lives of sin and self. The Lord God will not fill a dirty, polluted vessel. Paul said, "Let us cleanse ourselves from all filthiness of the flesh and spirit, perfecting holiness in the fear of God" (II Corinthians 7:1). You and I must be broken and spilled out for Him. God can fill in a moment what it takes years to empty. Elisha saw how God was able to use Elijah, the empty vessel. In absolute surrender, he cried out for a double portion of Elijah's spirit. Only God can take an empty vessel and fill it twice as full. He can do it for you and me if we will ask.

A pastor friend shared this poem by R.V. Cornwall with me when I visited his church in Pennsylvania. The original book is now out of print, but I would like to share it with you here.

Chosen Vessel

The Master was searching for a vessel to use,
Before Him were many, which one would He choose.

Take me cried the gold one, I'm shiny and bright,
I'm of great value and I do things just right.
My beauty and luster will outshine the rest

And for someone like you, Master, gold would be the best.

The Master passed on with no words at all,
And looked at a silver urn narrow and tall.
I'll serve you, dear Master, I'll pour out your wine.
I'll be on your table whenever you dine.
My lines are so graceful, my carving so true
And silver will always compliment you.

Then heeding, the Master passed on to the brass.
Wide mouth, shallow, and polished like glass.
You're here! Cried the vessel, I know I will do.
Place me on your table for all men to view.

Look at me, cried the goblet of crystal so clear.
My transparency shows my contents so dear.
Though fragile am I, I will serve you with pride
And I'm sure I'll be happy in your house to abide.

The Master came next to a vessel of wood,
Polished and carved it solidly stood.
You may use me dear Master the wooden bowl said,
But I'd rather you use me for fruit, not for bread.

Then the Master looked down and saw a bowl of clay,
Empty and broken it helplessly lay.
The hope had this vessel, that the Master might choose
To cleanse and make whole, to fill and to use.

Ah! This is the vessel I was hoping to find!
I'll mend it and use it and make it all mine.
I need not the vessel that is proud of itself,
Nor one that is there to sit on the shelf,

Nor one that is big mouthed, shallow and loud
Nor one that displays his content so proud.
Nor one who thinks he can do all things just right,
But this plain, earthly vessel filled with power and might.

Then gently He filled the vessel of clay,
Mended and cleansed it and filled it that day.
Spoke to it kindly, there's work you must do,
Just pour out to others as I pour into you.

As I reflect back on my life, I am astonished at the awesomeness of God. I realize how impossible it is for the finite minds of men to comprehend the infiniteness of the mind of God. In Isaiah 55:8-9 the Lord says, "For my thoughts are not your thoughts, neither are your ways my ways, saith the LORD. For as the heavens are higher than the earth, so are my ways higher than your ways, and my thoughts than your thoughts." Human rationale leaves me with the criteria for choosing a vessel—strong, appealing and costly. God chooses the ugly, feeble, frail vessel as R.V. Cornwall writes so beautifully in his poem.

We saw in Mark 6:8 that when the Lord sent the disciples out in ministry, He commanded them that they should ". . . take nothing for their journey, save a staff only; no scrip, no bread, no money in their purse." In 1976, I launched out with only a Rod in my hand, and it has been a great, long journey ever since. I am in my third decade of ministry. Each year, I realize more and more how dependent I am upon the Rod. It seems natural that as one becomes older and more experienced, he would become more independent. On the contrary, that is not true for the servant of God. The older I become, the more I realize with each passing year, that I desperately need God's Rod, the blessed and powerful Holy Spirit, working in and through my life. I can look back on many times during the early years of my ministry when I was tempted to throw down the rod and rush ahead of God in the power of my own flesh. Each instance was met with failure.

I have already mentioned the Monday morning when Becky, Eric, and I packed everything that we owned and headed to Lynchburg, Virginia. What I did not mention was what we found when we arrived there. From all I had heard, and from renditions I had seen in brochures, I envisioned and expected to step onto a glorious university campus. What we found instead was a barren mountain with a tent. This was Liberty Mountain? From that moment, God began to teach us that faith is believing something is so, when it is not so, so that it becomes so, because God said so! Hebrews 11:1 declares, "Now faith is the substance of things hoped for, the evidence of things not seen."

From the moment we arrived in Lynchburg, God began to make a way for us. He had indeed led us to this place, and multiplied memories of His goodness flood my mind. One of the first things God did was to lead us to a new apartment building that had been built to help struggling college students with families. After reviewing our financial history, the apartment managers told us that the government would be paying us $33.00 per month to live in that new apartment complex!

I had previously mentioned how God led me to assume the pastorate of Open Door Baptist Church in Tuscaloosa, Alabama, after I graduated from Liberty University. I did not mention that I assumed that pastorate after the church had just purchased a funeral home! A handful of us started that church in a funeral home, the place of the dead! Every time I would visit people and invite them to our church, I would ask, "Do you know where we are located?" They would say, "Oh, yes, we know where you are. You're located there at the funeral home." I would then respond, "Yes, but that place is no longer the place of the dead; that place has come alive!" I would then quote Revelation 1:18 where Jesus said, "I am he that liveth, and was dead; and, behold, I am alive for evermore, Amen; and have the keys of hell and of death."

Through the power of the Holy Spirit, God began to work in the life of each of us at Open Door Baptist Church. We began to grow. Our first edition to the church cost $40,000. We were able to raise that money and pay cash for the building. The next edition cost $250,000 and the next, a million dollars. Time after time we watched God, through the power of the Holy Spirit, meet every need we had. God took a little group of about 50 people and blessed our church with an active membership of 2,000. We watched Him enable us to build a Christian School of more than 300 and a daycare of over 100. God did great and mighty things as we walked with our Rod.

It is important to recognize that, as a result of Christ's redemptive work on Calvary, a new society was formed called the church. It was upon this group of people, Christ's own body, that the Holy Spirit descended at Pentecost to abide with, and in them, forever. The reality of the Spirit's presence is in the church. Just as it was on the day of Pentecost, so it is today. When you and I get saved, we are filled with the precious Holy Spirit, the Comforter. He is a living personality. This needs to be emphasized in our day. Erroneous teachings that discount or ignore the Holy Spirit as a person still exist. When you and I walk with our Rod, we walk with the living personality of God

Himself.

Not only do we see the reality of the Spirit's presence in the church, we see the authority of the Spirit's presence in the church. Acts 2:3-4 records that "There appeared unto them cloven tongues like as of fire, and it sat upon each of them. And they were all filled with the Holy Ghost, and began to speak with other tongues, as the Spirit gave them utterance." These words indicate that on the Day of Pentecost the Holy Spirit made the church His seat and His throne. In other words, the Holy Spirit is the ruler and administrator of all that we do in the church and in our lives. Andrew Murray has written:

> "The Holy Ghost is the director of the work of God upon the earth. And what we should do if we are to work rightly for God, and if God is to bless our work, is to see that we stand in a right relation to the Holy Ghost, that we give Him every day the place of honor that belongs to Him, and that in all our work and (what is more) in all our private inner life, the Holy Ghost shall always have the first place."[1]

The Holy Spirit instructs and teaches us in the way that we should go, and He guides us with His eyes (Psalm 32:8). It is He who will teach the leadership of the church. Speaking to the elders of Ephesus, Paul said, "Take heed therefore unto yourselves, and to all the flock, over the which the Holy Ghost hath made you overseers, to feed the church of God, which he hath purchased with his own blood" (Acts 20:28). Quite clearly then, the inauguration of the office of elders and overseers was not so much by the action of people as it was by divine appointment. The Rod of the Spirit sets aside those of us who were called to full-time ministry.

The Holy Spirit integrated the fellowship of the church on the Day of Pentecost. On that day the disciples were filled with the Holy Spirit, and then 3,000 souls were saved. These ". . . continued steadfastly in the apostles' doctrine and fellowship, and in breaking of bread, and in prayers" (Acts 2:42). This is the fellowship of the Spirit. As indicated in II Corinthians 13:14 and in Philippians 2:1, only the Holy Spirit can bring individual Christians into the unity of the Spirit and the bond of peace. From a Roman jail, Paul begged the Ephesians to ". . . walk worthy of the vocation wherewith ye are called, with all lowliness and meekness, with long-suffering, forbearing one another in love; Endeavoring to keep the unity of the Spirit in the bond of peace" (4:1-3). When we each walk with our Rod, the Holy Spirit, we have fellowship in the Body of Christ.

When a Christian or a church is prepared to submit to the authority of the Spirit, it will demonstrate the sufficiency of the Spirit. This is why Jesus promised the power of the Holy Spirit before He left for Heaven. He said, "Ye shall receive power, after that the Holy Ghost is come upon you" (Acts 1:8). The whole of the New Testament is a commentary on the little word, "power." In the Greek it is *dunamis*, a term from which we get the word "dynamite." In this one word is found all that the Christian needs for living, serving, or dying for Christ. The Holy Spirit ministers His sufficiency when He reveals the all-powerful Savior. Paul said, "For I am not ashamed of the gospel of Christ: for it is the power of God unto salvation to everyone that believeth; to the Jew first, and also to the Greek" (Romans 1:16). Here then is the power of God in Christ which works sufficiently to save the sinner through repentance, faith, and obedience. God's omnipotence is wrapped up in the Gospel; for at its very heart is the supreme message of a triumphantly risen Lord and Savior.

The Spirit reveals the all-powerful Sanctifier. Paul tells us, "For the preaching of the cross is to them that perish, foolishness; but unto us which are saved, it is the power of God" (I Corinthians 1:18). Our present, continuous, salvation is the work of sanctification. Christ, having reconciled us to God by His death, is now saving us by His life: "For if, when we were enemies, we were reconciled to God by the death of his Son; much more, being reconciled, we shall be saved by his life" (Romans 5:10).

The Spirit reveals the all-powerful Sovereign. Speaking of the second advent, Peter says, "For we have not followed cunningly devised fables, when we made known unto you the power and coming of our Lord Jesus Christ, but were eyewitnesses of his majesty" (II Peter 1:16). He speaks of a power that will not only purify us now, as we await that coming, but which will completely transform us when Jesus returns.

The Apostle Paul speaks of this when he says, "For our conversation (citizenship) is in heaven; from whence also we look for the Saviour, the Lord Jesus Christ: Who shall change our vile body, that it may be fashioned like unto his glorious body, according to the working whereby he is able even to subdue all things unto himself." (Philippians 3:20-21). What an experience that will be, when in a moment, in the twinkling of an eye, the trumpet will sound and the dead will be raised and changed (I Corinthian 15:52).

Can we think of any need that is not included in the power of the risen Christ and His saving, sanctifying, supervising ministry? All this and more is implied in the great concept of the presence of the Spirit in the Church

of Jesus Christ. Let us never forget that when we speak of
His presence, we are giving witness to His reality, authority,
and sufficiency in our lives. As we walk with the Rod
through our lives and ministries, God will reveal all that He
is through the power of the Holy Spirit.

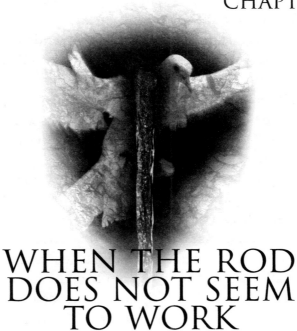

CHAPTER 8

WHEN THE ROD DOES NOT SEEM TO WORK

This entire work has been devoted to a study of God the Holy Spirit, the Third Person of the Trinity, who comes to indwell us at the time of our salvation. Our major focus has been upon the recognition of our desperate need for Spirit-anointed living. Although as Christians we are indwelt by the Holy Spirit, that does not automatically mean that we walk with and are controlled by our Rod. Without the empowering of the Holy Spirit, our works are fleshly, futile, and fruitless. We cannot live a fulfilled life unless we live under the Spirit's control. The symbolism we have studied thus far concerning the rod is meaningless unless applied and practiced in our lives. The concept of the "Rod of the Spirit" must be implemented in our daily walk with the Lord.

As we near the conclusion of this book, we must sober-
ly ask and answer the questions: Are the truths of the
abiding presence of the Holy Spirit relevant and realistic for
our lives today? Is it truly possible to be controlled by the
Holy Spirit so that we manifest the fruit of the Spirit and
see His power evident in our daily walk? I am confident
that a deeper understanding of these truths will revolu-
tionize our lifestyle, our relationship with the Lord, and
our ministry or area of service.

Many struggle today with the issue of how one becomes
"Spirit-filled," seeking to appropriate the power of God in
their personal lives and circumstances. There are certainly
no secret formulas that can be devised to ensure instanta-
neous success. It is necessary to establish useful guidelines
and biblical concepts that, when applied, result in a life of
victory. The Rod of the Spirit is not intended exclusively
for pastors, missionaries, or full-time Christian workers.
Every believer needs the anointing of God for victorious
Christian living and effectiveness in laboring in His fields.

The need of each Spirit-filled believer is for power to live
Godly and to perform each and every task appointed by the
Lord. For the teacher, power manifests itself in the form of
wisdom. Proverbs 2:6 states, "For the LORD giveth wisdom: out of his mouth cometh knowledge and understanding." For the singer, power manifests itself in an
anointed melody that stirs the listener. For the housewife,
it is the radiant love to make her house truly a home. For the
student, it is a fresh revelation of truth. For the laborer, it is
the quickening of the Spirit which brings a sense of God's
presence to the workplace. This power of the Holy Spirit is
not only for public service and ministry, but for private and
personal worship as well. The Bible says in John 4:23, "But
the hour cometh, and now is, when the true worshipers shall

worship the Father in spirit and in truth: for the Father seeketh such to worship him." God desires our worship, the only means by which we draw closer to Him.

One of the most important functions of the Spirit is to implant power for service within each believer. This power is made abundantly available to those who seek to be filled with God's Spirit. Paul verifies this in II Corinthians 4:7, "But we have this treasure in earthen vessels, that the excellence of the power may be of God and not of us." Although the ministry of the Holy Spirit encompasses a multitude of activities, this book is dedicated to what I believe is the most important facet of His ministry—the imparting of power for service. This hypothesis is substantiated by Paul in Ephesians 3:20 where he writes, "Now unto Him that is able to do exceeding abundantly above all that we ask or think, according to the power that worketh in us." The emphasis here is clearly upon the power of God. As we have seen, the word power in the Greek is *dunamis*, which is the origin of the word "dynamite." Within each believer there is this potential, explosive power just waiting to be unleashed.

What Paul gives us in Ephesians 3:20 is a great doxology of praise. When God has filled us with His fullness; when Christ's love has mastered us; and when the Holy Spirit has empowered us; then He is able to do exceedingly, abundantly above all that we ask or think. Until those conditions are met, God's working in us is limited. When they are met, His working in us is unlimited. As is frequently pointed out, verse 20 is a pyramid progression of God's enablement: He is able; He is able to do; He is able to do exceedingly, abundantly; He is able to do exceedingly, abundantly above all that we ask; He is able to do exceedingly, abundantly beyond all that we ask or think. There is no question that God is able to do far more than we can imagine or conceive. Too few Christians enjoy the privilege of seeing God do all that He wants to do in their lives because they fail to follow the pattern of enablement presented in these verses.

Jesus promised in John 14:12-14, "Verily, verily, I say unto you, He that believeth on me, the works that I do shall he do also; and greater works than these shall he do; because I go unto my Father. And whatsoever ye shall ask in my name, that will I do, that the Father may be glorified in the Son. If ye shall ask any thing in my name, I will do it." There are no circumstances or situations in which the Lord cannot use us, provided that we are submitted and yielded to Him. This involves death to the self-life. Paul knew what it was to be completely surrendered to God. The effectiveness of his ministry was that, "My speech and my preaching was not with enticing words of man's wisdom, but in demonstration of the Spirit and of power" (I Corinthians 2:4). "For the kingdom of God is not in word, but in power (I Corinthians 4:20).

Everything the Apostle Paul did was in and through the power of God. There was nothing that he could not see accomplished if it was in the Lord's will. There were certain things that were very important to Paul. He listed these in II Corinthians 6:3-7:

> "Giving no offense in any thing, that the ministry be not blamed: But in all things approving ourselves as the ministers of God, in much patience, in afflictions, in necessities, in distresses, In stripes, in imprisonments, in tumults, in labors, in watchings, in fastings; By pureness, by knowledge, by longsuffering, by kindness, by the Holy Ghost, by

> love unfeigned, By the word of truth, by the
> power of God, by the armor of righteousness
> onthe right hand and on the left."

According to Acts 1:8, this same power works in us by the presence of the Spirit. When you and I yield to God, He is able to do exceedingly, abundantly above all that we ask or think, according to the power that works within us. Only then are we truly effective, and only then is the Lord truly glorified. He deserves glory in the church now and forever.

Why are so many Christians seemingly oblivious to this truth about the Spirit's filling? Do they fail to recognize Him? Are they indifferent toward Him? Throughout my years of ministry, I have witnessed multitudes of Christians who have reached the frustration point. The Word of God has little visible effect in their lives. Every attempt to establish a fruitful, effective ministry seems to end in defeat. The rod they hold in their hands appears to be powerless. Still others build ministries, direct many to Christ, disciple, and motivate large numbers to service, and even perform miracles. I have observed men of God who expound and exhort the Word of God and enjoy the harvest of an outpouring of God's power. Their ability to handle God's Word with authority caused even the strongest of Satan's demons to flee their presence. I have seen the awareness of God's presence so prevalent that an entire audience was held spellbound.

On the opposite side of the coin, I have witnessed services which lacked the same power. Using a similar text and exhibiting what appeared to be a dynamic delivery, the pastor preached to seemingly deaf ears. Few were stirred, if any. Similarly, I have observed gospel musicians with finely tuned instruments present their music masterfully. Their singing was unequalled, and they produced a harmony that sounded forth as if it came from Heaven itself; yet there was no moving of God's Spirit.

Then I have been in services where average people with average talent ministered in music and shared personal testimonies. My heart has been stirred, and my cheeks have been warmed with tears. Why such a contrast? Why are some ministers of the gospel effective and powerful while others are ineffective and powerless? Why are some explosive like a stick of dynamite while others fizzle out like a wet firecracker? How can one preach with the fire of the Holy Spirit while the other becomes a smothering smoke screen?

There are three aspects which I consider imperative to obtaining power for service. The first prerequisite for acquiring this power is a genuine "born again" experience. Do not be so presumptuous as to believe that all who attempt to serve the Lord are born-again. Many well meaning, hard-working, sincere individuals have never truly been saved. There has never been a time and a place when they recognized their sinful, lost condition and called upon the name of Jesus Christ for salvation. They are sincerely zealous, but because they do not know Him personally, they have a form of godliness but demonstrate no power (II Timothy 3:5). This may seem an elementary truth, but there exists a multitude who ignore the biblical way to God and have sought Him through the conditions of men. Theirs is a salvation of works rather than one of faith. Let us never forget the words of Paul in Ephesians 2:8-10, "For by grace are ye saved through faith; and that not of yourselves: it is the gift of God: Not of works, lest any man should boast. For we are his workmanship, created in

Christ Jesus unto good works, which God hath before ordained that we should walk in them." Titus 3:5 confirms this, "Not by works of righteousness which we have done, but according to his mercy he saved us, by the washing of regeneration, and renewing of the Holy Ghost."

Jesus made it clear in John 15:5 that we can do nothing without Him, "I am the vine, ye are the branches. He that abideth in me, and I in him, the same bringeth forth much fruit; for without me ye can do nothing." An analogy is drawn between the grapevine and the Christian. Our Heavenly Father is the gardener or vinedresser, Jesus is the vine; and Christians are the branches of that vine. The branches that are to bear fruit are of no value to the gardener unless they are part of the vine. Certainly, branches cannot bear fruit independent of the tree. The tree is the source of supply which gives life. In order to produce, one must be in Christ. Productivity is dependent on the branch abiding in the vine. Are you truly attached to the vine who is Jesus?

John 15:4 states, "Abide in me, and I in you. As the branch cannot bear fruit of itself, except it abide in the vine; no more can ye, except ye abide in me." Our union with Christ is a living union so that we may bear fruit. It is a loving union so that we may enjoy Him. It is a lasting union so that we need not be afraid. As a branch by itself, we are weak and useless, good for burning but not for building. The branch cannot produce its own life; it must draw its life from the vine. It is our communion with Christ as a Spirit that makes possible the bearing of the fruit.

So we see that Scripture makes it clear that there must be union and communion. The Bible is replete with this critical concept. We see this in the body and its members (I Corinthians 12); the bride and the bridegroom

(Ephesians 5:25-33); and the sheep and the shepherd (John 10). A member of the body cut off from the body dies. The marriage creates the union, but it takes daily love and devotion to maintain communion. The shepherd brings the sheep into the flock, but the sheep must follow the shepherd in order to have protection and provision. The sooner we as believers discover the truth of our position as branches, the better we will relate to the Lord. We will know our weakness and confess our need for His strength.

An important word and a key concept used eleven times in John 15:1-11 is the word "abide." Synonyms include the words "continue" in John 15:9 and "remain" in John 15:11. What does it mean to abide? It means to keep in fellowship with Christ so that His life can work in and through us to produce fruit. This certainly involves the Word of God and the confession of sin so that nothing hinders our communion with Him (John 15:3). It also involves obeying Him because we love Him (John 15:9-10).

How can we tell when we are abiding in Christ? Is there a special feeling? Not really. There are, however, special evidences that appear and are unmistakably clear. Those who abide in Christ produce fruit. That fruit is a living testimony of what Christ is in the believer's life. Also, one experiences the Father's pruning so that he will bear more fruit (John 15: 2). The believer who is abiding in Christ has his prayers answered (John 15:7). He experiences a deep love for Christ and other believers (John 15:9, 12-13). He also experiences an unbelievable joy (John 15:11). This abiding relationship is natural to the branch and the vine, but it must be cultivated in the Christian life. It is not automatic. Abiding in Christ requires worship, study and meditation of God's Word, prayer, sacrifice, and service. What a joyful experience it is! Once a believer begins to cultivate this unbelievable relationship of union and communion with Christ, he has no desire to return to the shallow life of the carnal, careless Christian.

For the Rod to work and be mighty in our lives, we must be sure of our calling. I am fully persuaded that every believer has a specific purpose and calling. God saved you to place you in the Body of Christ as a specific member with a specific function. Romans 12:6 says, "Having then gifts differing according to the grace that is given to us." Paul too stresses in this chapter that every member of the Body of Christ is given a particular gift of function. Some are given the ability to teach, while others are given the gifts of faith, hospitality, giving, showing mercy, helps, etc. There are many and varied spiritual gifts bestowed on Christians according to God's choosing. I will not proceed into an indepth study on the spiritual gifts. Suffice it is to say that you must discover through much prayer and communion with the Father what your position of calling includes. II Peter 1:10 states, "Wherefore the rather, brethren, give diligence to make your calling and election sure: for if ye do these things, ye shall never fall."

I sincerely believe that many Christians experience failure because they attempt to operate outside the realm of their particular calling or gifting. God has chosen you to be a special part of His body. Do not allow yourself to be dislocated by improper use. Do not try to perform in areas of ministry to which God has not called or equipped you to serve. When we become willing to serve in the specific area of our calling, He will supply the necessary power to perform the task. Serving within the boundaries of God's calling will bring success and contentment. Trying to perform outside your specific calling will only lead to failure and frustration. Christians, like athletes, must learn to play their position. Each participant is assigned to the position that best fits his capability. Each member, doing what he does best, results in teamwork and success for the entire team or body. A one-man basketball or football team is destined to fail. It behooves us as Christians to learn to play a position and be satisfied that God has chosen us for that position. Not all Christians are singers, songwriters, preachers, teachers, or missionaries. Few have the ability to write and sing like Bill and Gloria Gaither. Nor can we all preach like Billy Graham. We are assured that the Spirit equally distributes spiritual gifts to every man separately as He wills (I Corinthians 12:11).

Let me share with you what can happen to one who tries to function outside his gifting and calling. A man I met thought he was called to preach because of a comment made to him at the church where he served. He had gotten on fire for God, and someone had said, "Oh, you must be called to preach!" Because of that statement and the excitement he had experienced, this man left his job as a respiratory therapist and went to Liberty University to study for the ministry. After he left Liberty University, he went to Mobile, Alabama, to start a church. Open Door Baptist Church helped underwrite that man's ministry.

For years the church struggled and did not do well. Finally the man called me and said, "I don't know if I'm really called to be a pastor. Maybe I am supposed to be a Christian educator." To help this man, we allowed him to come to our growing Christian school and be its headmaster. After four frustrating and unfulfilled years of discontent, he came to the realization that God had not called him into full-time ministry. He saw that God had really called him to be a respiratory therapist. This is where he had been a great witness as he exercised his gift of mercy.

He also realized that God wanted him to be a servant and use his gift of teaching within the local church.

When Richard left full-time ministry he had felt frustrated, defeated, and forsaken. But God allowed Richard to get another full-time job as a respiratory therapist in the same hospital where he had previously worked. To this day, he is still working there and serving in his local church. He experiences victory instead of defeat because he is serving in the area of his giftedness and calling. This powerful Rod held in his hand as a preacher or administrator was ineffective, but the Rod held in his hand as a respiratory therapist produced a powerful witness for the Lord. Like Richard, we each must seek out our specific place of service and produce the fruit of God's choosing.

Many so-called preachers in the ministry today are really man-called. No wonder there is no fruit, no power, and no presence of an awesome and real God in their midst. Let us never forget the words of Paul in II Timothy 1:9, "Who hath saved us, and called us with a holy calling, not according to our works, but according to his own purpose and grace, which was given us in Christ Jesus before the world began." Timothy knew he was ". . . appointed a preacher, and an apostle, and a teacher of the Gentiles" (II Timothy 1:11). The Lord Jesus Christ has saved us and given us special gifts, abilities, and talents for a specific task that He has chosen for us. Let us seek God's will and calling that we might bring Him the greatest glory.

For the Rod to work effectively there must be purity in heart and motive. In II Kings 4:18-37, there is a most unusual order of events. The Shunammite woman who had been so gracious and kind to Elisha in furnishing him a room, experienced tragedy in her life. Her only son fell sick one day while working in the field and later died in his mother's arms. Without hesitation, the Shunammite woman sought out Elisha, the man of God. In verse 27 we read that she fell at Elisha's feet weeping bitterly as she explained to him that her only son was dead. Then in the preceding verses we find Elisha giving his staff or rod to his servant Gehazi and commissioning him to go to the boy and lay the staff upon his face. Gehazi did this, but Scripture tells us, ". . . there was neither voice, nor hearing. Wherefore he went again to meet him (Elisha), and told him, saying, The child is not awaked" (31). Elisha went alone into the child's room, shut the door, and prayed. Then he stretched himself upon the child, and life was immediately restored to him. The joyous mother fell at Elisha's feet, bowed herself to the ground, took up her son, and went out.

It seems puzzling that the staff, the rod, in the hand of Gehazi was worthless and accomplished nothing. To gain understanding, we must go to II Kings 5. There we see the sin that was in Gehazi's life. In this chapter, we find Naaman, captain of the host of the king of Syria coming to Elisha to receive healing of his leprosy. He came proudly with money and clothing to pay for his healing. Through a messenger, Elisha instructed the captain to go to the Jordan River and dip himself in it seven times to effect his healing. At first Naaman was filled with rage at such a suggestion, but his servants begged him to obey the man of God which he finally did. He was instantly healed. Elisha refused any payment, desiring that Naaman know his healing was totally credited to the grace of God. Gehazi, however, in his greed ran after Naaman and lied to him, telling him that visitors had arrived and that Elisha did indeed desire some silver two changes of clothes.

Obviously Gehazi was not the man of God that Elisha

was. The problem was not with the staff but with his heart. I like what the Psalmist says in Psalm 139: 23-24, "Search me, O God, and know my heart: try me, and know my thoughts: And see if there be any wicked way in me, and lead me in the way everlasting." We render ourselves useless in the service of God if there is sin in our lives. The Psalmist said in Psalm 66:18, "If I regard iniquity in my heart, the Lord will not hear me." Why do people think that the Word of God fails? Why do they think that prayers go unanswered? Why are so few souls saved? Why are churches so dead? Why is there no power? We pick up the rod, shake it a few times, throw it aside and say, "Crazy stick, it just doesn't work!" The problem, however, is not with the rod. The problem is with us.

Often a failing ministry is met with cries of desperation for new methods. We make excuses. "These people are just different," we lament. "This is a difficult area in which to minister." We reach for a new ministry, an improved music program, or the addition of outings and socials. The list could go on and on. Equipment helps, but it is incidental. It is useful to the pastor, but not vital. The best boat or outdoor motor will not make a man a fisherman. The best airplane developed will not make a man a pilot. Having the best tools available does not make one a good carpenter. Generators and modern electrical devices may brighten mission stations, but they can never bring light out of spiritual darkness. One may be attired in the finest clothes but never bring the hope of righteousness to heathen hearts. The best radio will not enable a man to hear from heaven. The finest medical training and equipment will not heal the brokenhearted. Before discarding the Rod if it seems to fail, examine your life, heart, and motive. Let us not forget, "For as he thinketh in his heart, so is he" (Proverbs 23:7).

That is why he says in Proverbs 23:26, "My son, give me thine heart, and let thine eyes observe my ways."

In Luke 4 we find insight regarding the anointing of the Holy Spirit of God. I believe that the key to that anointing is a life of holiness. In relation to His God, Jesus was holy. In relation to his fellow man, he was harmless. His life was completely free from any malice. We find in Luke 3:22 at Jesus' baptism that, "The Holy Ghost descended in a bodily shape like a dove upon him, and a voice came from heaven, which said, 'Thou art my beloved Son; in thee am I well-pleased.'" Hebrews 7:26 says, "For such an high priest became us, who is holy, harmless, undefiled, separate from sinners, and made higher than the heavens."

As was true of Jesus, our lives, too, must be free of malice (Ephesians 4:29, Luke 23:34). Jesus was undefiled. He was spotless, unstained, a lamb without blemish and without spot. We also are to be spotless and unstained. How can we do this? Probably a better question would be, "How can we not do this when we think of the promise of II Corinthians 6:18, "I will be a Father unto you, and ye shall be my sons and daughters, saith the Lord Almighty." How can I disappoint a loving heavenly Father who has promised to live His life out through mine in the blessedness of the Holy Spirit? "Having therefore these promises, dearly beloved, let us cleanse ourselves from all filthiness of the flesh and spirit, perfecting holiness in the fear of God" (II Corinthians 7:1)

Because God the Holy Spirit lives in me, I must ". . . have no fellowship with the unfruitful works of darkness, but rather reprove them" (Ephesians 5:11). You and I must be holy to be anointed. This involves growth in the grace and knowledge of our Lord and Savior, Jesus Christ (II Peter 3:18). The anointing is also a gift as we have seen before in

I John 2:27, "But the anointing which ye have received of him abideth in you, and ye need not that any man teach you; but as the same anointing teacheth you of all things, and is truth, and is no lie, and even as it hath taught you, ye shall abide in him." A growth, a gift, and a goal are that we be holy. We are commanded, "Be ye holy in all manner of conversation; Because it is written, 'Be ye holy; for I am holy'" (I Peter 1: 15-16). We must keep sin out of our hearts so that the Holy Spirit can fill us.

The anointing not only involves a life of holiness, but it involves a life of yieldedness. Is your heart attitude one of complete yieldedness to God? Are you a slave of the Lord Jesus, with no mind or will of your own? Have you given your all to the Master? Can you say, "I am totally yours, Lord. All that I am and all that I have is yours to do with as you see fit." It takes total yieldedness in our lives to effect total obedience. If we hold back a part of our lives, it is impossible to know victory in obedience. Although Jesus was sinless, he willingly yielded to baptism, explaining to the hesitant John, "Suffer it to be so now: for thus it becometh us to fulfill all righteousness" (Matthew 3:15). In the Garden of Gethsemane, Jesus asked if it was possible that He could forgo the horrors of the cross, ". . . nevertheless, not my will, but thine, be done" (Luke 22:42). Jesus was totally yielded to the Father no matter what the personal cost. When we are totally yielded to the Lord, obedience is a natural consequence.

Prayerfulness must come along with holiness and yieldedness. Jesus certainly made prayer a priority in His life while He was on this earth. "Now when all the people were baptized, it came to pass, that Jesus also being baptized, and praying, the heaven was opened" (Luke 3:21). Jesus said that ". . . men ought always to pray, and not to faint" (Luke 18:1).

What is the cure for worry? "Rejoice in the Lord always: and again I say, Rejoice. Be careful for nothing; but in every thing by prayer and supplication with thanksgiving let your requests be made known unto God. And the peace of God, which passeth all understanding, shall keep your hearts and minds through Christ Jesus" (Philippians 4:4,6-7). I have seen surveys that indicate that the average time a preacher spends in prayer preparing for a sermon is less than two minutes. No wonder we hear powerless sermons. Paul said, "Pray without ceasing. In every thing give thanks: for this is the will of God in Christ Jesus concerning you" (1 Thessalonians 5:17-18). As we walk with our Rod in prayer, we will see the power of the Holy Spirit manifested in our lives and ministries. We will realize God working through us.

I have been in many churches all across this country that spare no expense or effort on appearance, but inside there is no power. All the paraphernalia looks and sounds nice, but there is no power to move it. Millions, and even billions of dollars, are spent on glass cathedrals, plush carpets, stained glass windows, padded pews, and sound equipment. The pastors are dignified professional men with many degrees. The candles are burning brightly; the choir is in perfect harmony; and the program is working to perfection, but there is no anointing. We know when to stand, when to sit, when to kneel, and when to say "amen." There are preludes, postludes, and interludes which look impressive and sound good, but there is no anointing or power.

It is not by the eloquence, education, or administrative skills of man that mighty works are accomplished for God; it is by the power and anointing of the Holy Spirit. Remember Zechariah 4:6 says, "This is the word of the LORD . . . Not by might, nor by power, but by my spirit, saith the LORD of hosts." At Pentecost Jesus told his disciples that they were to receive the Holy Spirit and power. Before Pentecost they were not able to walk in the calling Jesus committed to them. Each demonstrated greed, fear, anxiety, doubt, anger, carnality, pride, and a host of other sinful, unprofitable deeds of the flesh. But what a difference there was in these men after Pentecost! They had boldness and power to stand firmly in their testimonies. The power of evil forces was broken, and the spiritual captives were released from bondage. The power of the flesh and carnal deeds no longer controlled them. The same Peter who denied his Lord and cursed Him, preached a sermon on the Day of Pentecost that resulted in the salvation of more than 3,000 people. Throughout the rest of his life, Peter demonstrated zeal and boldness that characterized him until the day he was martyred. I believe God purposely chose to use the disciples lives to demonstrate the difference that Pentecost made. They were saved and under the blood but were not effective in their ministries until after the Holy Spirit came into their hearts and lives in His wondrous fullness.

May we see the heart of God today. He longs for us, His children, to live intimately with Him that we might experience life abundantly. An abundant life is one characterized by love, joy, peace, long-suffering, gentleness, goodness, faith, meekness, and self-control. It is a victorious and fruitful life of service. II Peter 1:3 tells us that, "According as his divine power hath given unto us all things that pertain unto life and godliness, through the knowledge of him that hath called us to glory and virtue." He has provided everything we need to live a life of victory and service. That life is only possible as we walk with our Rod daily. R. Kent Hughes has written:

"Where the Spirit reigns, believers relate to the Word—teaching.

Where the Spirit reigns, believers relate to each other—koinonia.

Where the Spirit reigns, believers relate to God—worship.

Where the Spirit reigns, believers relate to the world—evangelism."[1]

We who are believers since Pentecost have been given God the Holy Spirit to live within us. He is our Guide, our Teacher, our Helper, our Comforter, and so much more. He reveals to us the mind of Christ and the will of God. He anoints us with power for service to the King. What a privilege and an honor to have Him live within us! May we seek Him and know Him in His fullness that we might bring God glory on this earth. Then when we enter that great eternal Kingdom of our Lord, we will be able to lay many crowns at the feet of Jesus and hear Him say, "Well done, thou good and faithful servant; enter into the joy of your lord." Matthew 25:21

ENDNOTES

Introduction

[1] A.W. Tozier, *When He Is Come* (Camp Hill, Pennsylvania: Christian Publications, 1968).

Chapter Two

[1] Phillip Keller, *A Shepherd Looks at Psalm 23* (Grand Rapids, Michigan: Zondervan Publishing House, 1970), 100-101, 103.

Chapter Three

[1] Translated by Edward B. Pusey, D.D., *The Confessions of Saint Augustine*, (New York: The Modern Library, 1999), 196, 144.

[2] Dr. & Mrs. Howard Taylor, *Hudson Taylor's Spiritual Secret* (Chicago: Moody Press, 1989), 6-7.

[3] Dr. & Mrs. Howard Taylor, *Hudson Taylor's Spiritual Secret* (Chicago: Moody Press, 1989), 19-20.

[4] Andrew Murray, *Absolute Surrender* (Chicago: Moody Press, 1987), 8.

[5] Andrew Murray, *Absolute Surrender* (Chicago: Moody Press, 1987), 11-12.

Chapter Four

[1] Andrew Murray, *Absolute Surrender* (Chicago: Moody Press,, 1987), 79.

Chapter Five

[1] Gleason L. Archer, *Encyclopedia of Bible Difficulties* (Grand Rapids, Michigan: Zondervan Publishing House, 1982).

Chapter Six

[1] Dan B. Allender, Ph.D., *The Healing Path* (Colorado Springs, Colorado: WATERBROOK PRESS, 1999), 123.

Chapter Seven

[1] Andrew Murray, *Absolute Surrender* (Chicago: Moody Press, 1987), 44.

Chapter Eight

[1] R. Kent Hughes, *1001 Great Stories & Quotes* (Wheaton, Illinois: Tyndale House Publishers, Inc., 1998), 207.